GREAT AMERICAN ROAD TRIPS
Hidden Gems

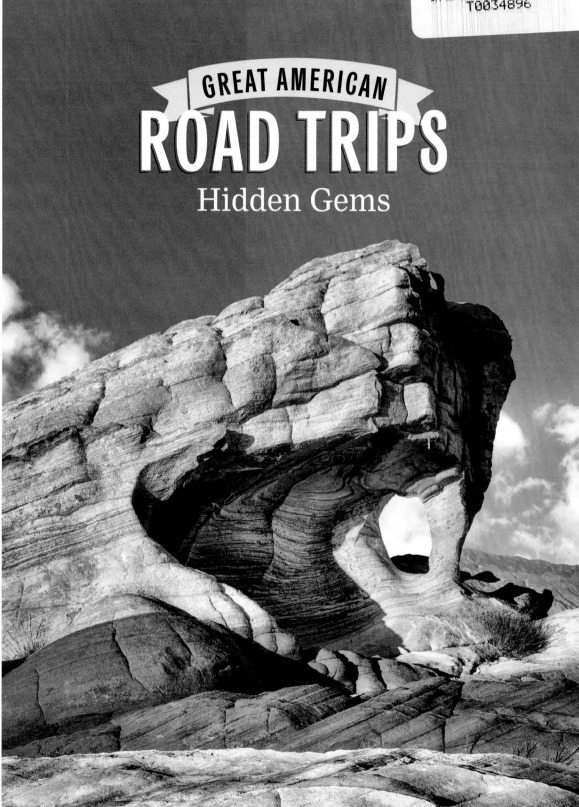

▼

The power of wind and water formed Fire Canyon Arch at Valley of Fire State Park in Nevada.

▼

When it's below freezing, ice sculptures form at Cave Point County Park, a symbol of Door County, Wisconsin.

© 2021 RDA Enthusiast Brands, LLC.
1610 N. 2nd St., Suite 102
Milwaukee, WI 53212-3906

ISBN
978-1-62145-592-9 (Hardcover)
978-1-62145-593-6 (Paperback)

COMPONENT NUMBER
116500104H

We are committed to both the quality of our products
and the service we provide to our customers.
We value your comments, so please feel free to contact
us at *TMBBookTeam@TrustedMediaBrands.com*.

For more *Country* products and information,
visit our website: *www.country-magazine.com*

Printed in U.S.A.
1 3 5 7 9 10 8 6 4 2 (Hardcover)
1 3 5 7 9 10 8 6 4 2 (Paperback)

PICTURED ON FRONT COVER
Boardwalk at Empire Bluff Overlook, Sleeping Bear Dunes
National Lakeshore, Michigan, by Aubrieta V. Hope

ILLUSTRATIONS Anna Simmons

ADDITIONAL PHOTO INFORMATION
Pages 8-9: Rainbow Falls, Devils Postpile National Monument,
California, by Alan Tan/Getty Images
Pages 64-65: Chiricahua National Monument, Arizona,
by Brent Loe Photography
Pages 86-87: Sleeping Bear Dunes National Lakeshore,
Michigan, by Robert Du Bois/Getty Images
Pages 122-123: Atchafalaya Basin, Louisiana,
by Michael Lustbader/Image Finders
Pages 168-169: West Cornwall Covered Bridge, Litchfield County,
Connecticut, Courtesy of Connecticut Office of Tourism

Text, photography and illustrations for *Great American
Road Trips: Hidden Gems* are based on articles previously
published in *Country* magazine (*www.country-magazine.com*).

CONTENTS

A pair of roseate spoonbills quarrel with each other on Jefferson Island, Louisiana. ◄

MOUNT

PACIFIC OCEAN

Baker-Snoqualmie

Wallowa Lake

BIGHORN
MOUNTAINS

SAWTOOTH MOUNTAINS ★
★ LOST RIVER RANGE
& LEMHI MOUNTAIN
RANGE

CAMAS PRAIRIE
CENTENNIAL MARSH ★

W E S T

SHASTA-
TRINITY ★

W E S T

GRAND
STAIRCASE-ESCALANTE

Northern
RIO
GRANDE

Devils
POSTPILE

VALLEY OF
FIRE
★

S O U T H W E S T

CHANNEL ISLANDS ★

★ VERDE
VALLEY

PALO
DURO
CANYON

ORGAN
PIPE
CACTUS

CHIRICAHUA
★

CHUGACH

Arrowhead

DOOR COUNTY

NORTHERN WISCONSIN WATERFALLS

PIPESTONE

SILOS & SMOKESTACKS

MIDWEST

SLEEPING BEAR DUNES

NORTHEAST

TULLY LAKE

BIRCH HILL

THE GREAT SWAMP

Litchfield Hills

PINE CREEK Gorge

APPALACHIAN FOREST

Flint Hills

RED RIVER GORGE

BURKE'S GARDEN

LINVILLE GORGE WILDERNESS

ATLANTIC

CATALOOCHEE VALLEY

NEWTON COUNTY

SOUTHEAST

WAKULLA SPRINGS

GULLAH GEECHEE

ATCHAFALAYA BASIN

COASTAL CONNECTION Scenic Byway

OCEAN

Kayaking and fishing are favorite pastimes on the pristine waters of Oregon's Wallowa Lake.

TIME FOR A GETAWAY

IF YOU PICKED UP THIS BOOK, then you are ready for a trip! Whether near or far, you are dreaming of the perfect destination. And we're here to help!

Discover some of the most beautiful places in America that you might never have heard of before in the pages of *Great American Road Trips: Hidden Gems.* This book is the third in the series and features engaging firsthand travel accounts with helpful advice and stunning images taken by many of America's best scenic photographers.

You'll find easy-to-get-to road trips that are a bit off the beaten path, organized by region of the country. Some trips offer activities for the more adventurous, such as rafting or mountain biking; others include suggestions for the more leisurely traveler who wants to stop and take in the views by the roadside.

The small towns and people you'll encounter along the way will certainly leave their mark. Take, for instance, the Sea Islands culture of the Gullah Geechee along the southeastern coast of the United States. And do you know how Burke's Garden, Virginia, got its name? Or maybe you are seeking wildlife; we've got you covered with locations such as the Channel Islands in California. Let this book help you set the agenda for your next getaway.

So get ready to jump in the car or RV and share these experiences with the ones you love!

—FROM THE EDITORS

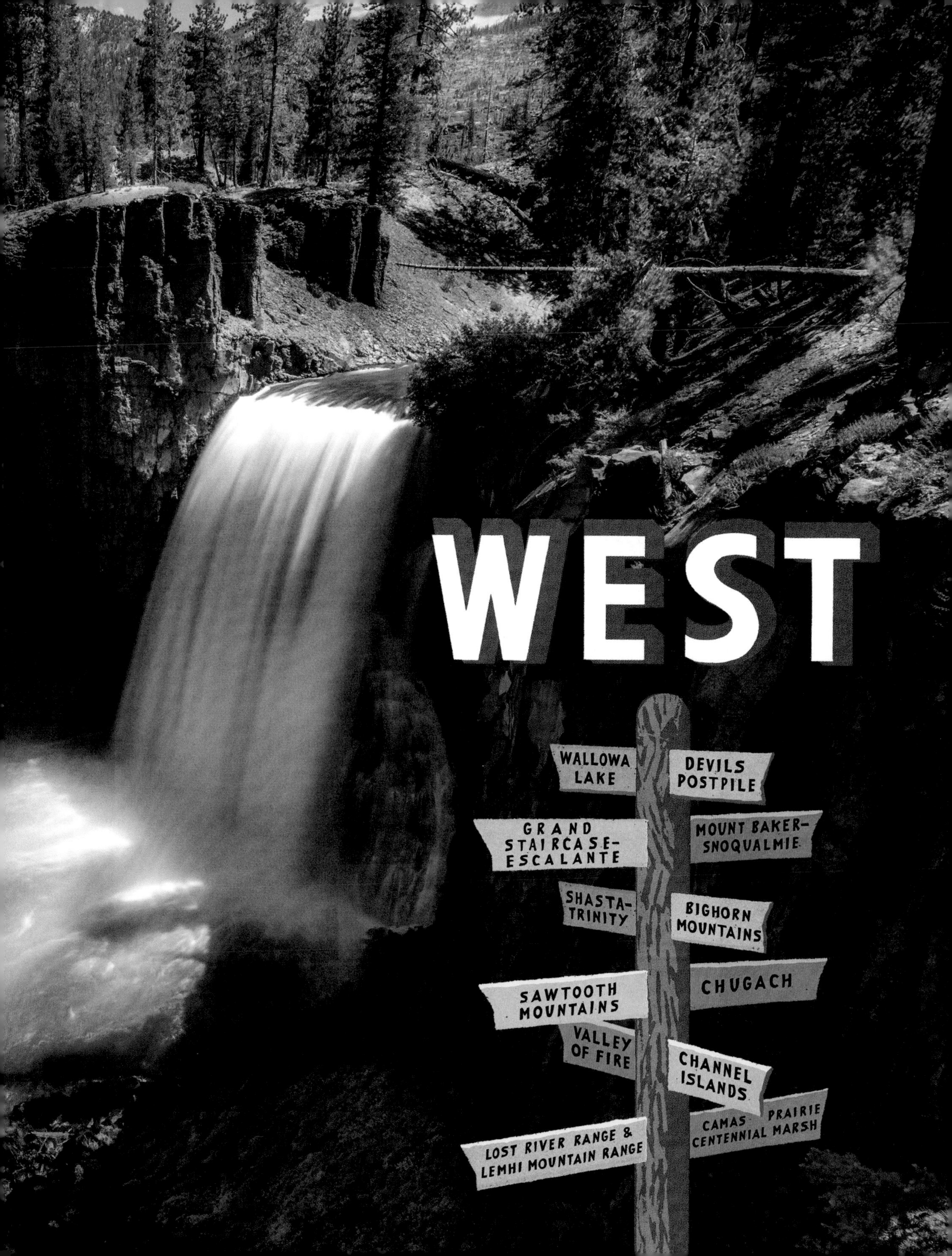

WEST

WALLOWA LAKE

DEVILS POSTPILE

GRAND STAIRCASE-ESCALANTE

MOUNT BAKER-SNOQUALMIE

SHASTA-TRINITY

BIGHORN MOUNTAINS

SAWTOOTH MOUNTAINS

CHUGACH

VALLEY OF FIRE

CHANNEL ISLANDS

LOST RIVER RANGE & LEMHI MOUNTAIN RANGE

CAMAS PRAIRIE CENTENNIAL MARSH

▼

Wildflowers bloom at the foot of Spencer Glacier.

Alaska

STORY BY **JANINE NIEBRUGGE**
PHOTOS BY **RON NIEBRUGGE**

CHUGACH

EASY TRAILS LEAD TO GORGES, GLACIERS AND GRAND VISTAS IN AMERICA'S SECOND-LARGEST NATIONAL FORESTLAND.

OVERSHADOWED BY DENALI National Park to the north, Alaska's Chugach National Forest flies below the radar of many visitors. The beautifully diverse Chugach is home to scores of glaciers and ice fields, lush rainforests and magnificent mountain ranges that descend to meet the ocean.

My husband, Ron, and I spend a lot of time hiking, photographing, trail running, cross-country skiing and camping in Chugach, which is about the size of New Hampshire yet only has 90 miles of Forest Service roads.

Although much of the massive national forest is not easily accessible, there are many fascinating areas to visit—and some are surprisingly simple to reach.

Near the town of Girdwood, a 45-minute drive along the Seward Highway from Anchorage, you can find yourself hiking in the beautiful rainforest on the Winner Creek Trail. The easiest way to reach the trail is from the Alyeska Resort, and the first half-mile is accessible to the disabled. Farther down the trail you'll be treated

NOT TO BE MISSED

Among the many lakes dotting Chugach's millions of acres are Lower Summit Lake and then Summit Lake, a bit to the south. Lower Summit Lake lures nature photographers seeking exemplary shots of wildflowers.

FUN FACT

There are about 100,000 glaciers in Alaska, and the beautiful blue color associated with them is created by the density of the ice, which absorbs all the colors of the spectrum except blue, which is reflected.

SIDE TRIP

Chugach State Park encompasses a half-million acres of forest, mountains and glaciers. Visit the Potter Section House, a restored building once occupied by railroad workers who maintained tracks here during the days of steam locomotives. Declared a state historic site, the structure is home to the Chugach State Park headquarters.

▼

Fishing boats crowd the harbor in Cordova.

to an impressive gorge and a hand tram to cross the creek. This is one of my favorite places to take visitors, as the trail is a fairly easy hike and a pathway to some marvelous views.

Right in our backyard in Seward is Lost Lake Trail, one of Ron's favorite places to photograph and an area where I spend countless hours year-round. The trail runs through landscapes from the verdant rain forest to alpine meadows full of summer wildflowers. Hardy hikers who break above the tree line to alpine tundra discover delightful alpine ponds and pristine Lost Lake.

A truly wonderful place to visit is the tiny coastal community of Cordova, which is surrounded by the Chugach forest and has access points to many trails. Located along Prince William Sound at the mouth of the Copper River, Cordova is accessible only by boat or plane. I try to make at least one trip a year there via the Alaska State Ferry.

Another option around Cordova is to venture into picturesque Prince William Sound and kayak in fjords surrounded by awe-inspiring tidewater glaciers.

My favorite time of year to visit Cordova is early May, when tens of thousands of migrating shorebirds stop in the area to feed. It's breathtaking to stand on the shore and watch these birds flock together in a kind of rhythmic pattern to music only they seem to hear.

A trip to Spencer Glacier is a must. It's a place where I love to camp, but if camping isn't your thing or you don't have that kind of time, no problem—the Alaska Railroad can take you on a day trip from Anchorage to this remote location. A short 1.3-mile hike on a groomed gravel trail takes you to the shores of Spencer Lake, where you can enjoy views of this beautiful glacier in all its glory.

I'd recommend a visit in mid- to late July, when blooming fireweed creates the most stunning scene imaginable. Extend your hike another 2 miles and you'll find yourself at the base of Spencer Glacier.

Chugach is also home to abundant wildlife. Bald eagles find the perfect habitat along the shores of Prince William Sound. Moose, deer, black bears and grizzly bears can also be seen in the forest.

Whether you spend a day or a lifetime in Chugach National Forest, there's a world of beauty to see and places to explore. And make very sure you don't forget your camera! ◾

A grizzly bear ◄ prowls slowly through Chugach's verdant rainforest.

▼
Hiking this trail on Santa Cruz Island offers lovely views of Potato Harbor.

STORY BY
AMELIA MULARZ

CHANNEL ISLANDS

A DAY IN THE WILD SEARCHING FOR UNIQUE WILDLIFE IN
CALIFORNIA'S OFF-THE-COAST NATIONAL PARK.

"THAT, LADIES AND GENTLEMEN, is our third humpback whale!" the ferry captain announces. *That's great*, I think to myself. But what I'd really like to see today is a fox.

You know it's an epic day for wildlife sightings when you take mighty whales for granted. It is not that I am not impressed by the massive marine life, but today's adventure is unique. That is, I'm looking for wildlife that exists nowhere else on Earth. My destination? Channel Islands National Park, often called the Galapagos of North America. Made up of five volcanic islands that are completely isolated despite their relative proximity to mainland California (the closest island is just

14 miles off the coast of Ventura), the park is home to 145 plants and animals you can't find anywhere else.

For my journey, I'm cruising with Island Packers, the ferry service that partners with the park. Channel Islands can be reached only by boat or plane, which explains why it's one of the least-visited national parks despite its jaw-dropping beauty (fields of yellow coreopsis flowers meet sheer rock faces, secluded beaches are tucked within craggy coves and crystal clear waters reveal clusters of purple sea anemones below). If you've got an ample budget, you can fly with Channel Islands Aviation or charter a private boat, but most visitors climb aboard

POINTS of INTEREST

WORDS TO THE WISE

Each of the five islands has one basic campground. Reserve sites at *recreation. gov* at least 6 months in advance. Pack plenty to eat and drink, as you won't find services on the islands and some don't have drinking water. Enclosed gas stoves are allowed, but campfires are not. Pack out whatever you took in. Campsites don't have trash cans.

Ferries to the islands leave from either Channel Islands Harbor in Oxnard or Ventura Harbor, depending on your destination.

NEARBY ATTRACTIONS

Dig in to fish and chips at Sea Fresh, *seafreshci.com*, in Oxnard, or slurp oysters at Brophy Bros. in Ventura, *brophybrosventura. com*. Peruse produce at Channel Islands Harbor Farmers Market. Or grab a souvenir at Ventura Harbor Village, *channelislands harbor.org*. Peep at a tide pool exhibit, learn about the indigenous Chumash culture or chat with a ranger at the visitor center in Ventura.

▼

The island scrub-jay is found exclusively on Santa Cruz Island.

the ferries, which leave out of either Ventura or Oxnard, both about an hour north of Los Angeles.

Today, I'm headed to Santa Cruz, the largest and most biologically diverse of the islands, which is ideal for my wildlife pursuits. Santa Cruz is also home to Painted Cave, a colorful sea formation that is beloved by both snorkelers and kayakers. The other islands have their draws, too. Anacapa, the closest to the mainland, is known for its iconic rock arch and historic lighthouse. Rare Torrey pines can be found on Santa Rosa, and San Miguel has a fossilized forest plus one of the largest rookeries of seals and sea lions in the world. Lastly, Santa Barbara is a cliff island with superb water visibility for underwater diving.

"Turn toward 3 o'clock," the captain's voice booms over the speaker. "That's what's called a nursery pod—dozens of baby dolphins."

I've been so focused on what I'll see on the island, I haven't considered that the 90-minute ferry ride is a wildlife show in itself. As for what I'm hoping to spot on Santa Cruz, I'm on the lookout for two creatures that are endemic, or unique, to these isles: the island fox and the island scrub-jay. The fox, which was on the brink of extinction in the early 2000s, is one-third smaller than its mainland relatives, while the scrub-jay is one-third larger than its continental counterpart and a darker blue.

Soon, we pull up to the island and dock at Prisoners Harbor, the port of entry to the park. After a brief orientation with a ranger, I beeline to the Pelican Bay hiking trail. I've been told this 4-mile (round-trip) coastal trek will give me the best shot at spotting my furry and feathered friends, though the ranger does point out that the fox will be the bigger challenge of the two.

The trail is narrow and winds through what feels like half a dozen different ecosystems. I spy wetlands and dense shrubbery with manzanita trees, then scramble down a rugged decline into a canyon before climbing uphill to take in a cacti-dotted field and ocean views. It's no wonder the Channel Islands play host to such fantastic flora—the list reads like something from a whimsical children's book (sticky monkey-flower and live forever) or a dessert menu (bush mallow and cream cups).

Still no foxes or scrub-jays as I reach Pelican Bay, which has a storybook quality of its own. Santa Cruz actually served as the backdrop for Never-Never Land scenes in the 1924 film *Peter Pan*. As I leave to double back on the trail, I hear a tiny squeak from an island deer mouse, also endemic to the area. I watch as he struggles to climb a small mound of volcanic rock, and I decide that he's the hardest working mouse in California (sorry, Mickey!).

▼

The park is a diving destination with kelp forests and Garibaldi fish.

▼
Anacapa Island was once called Ennepah, or mirage, due to its changing shape when viewed from the mainland.

Amelia's search for the elusive island fox led to wildlife sightings all over the park.

I'm now nearing the three-quarter mark of the hike and begin to fear I'll never see the distinctive duo. I slow my pace and alternate scanning the ground and treetops obsessively. Every rustling leaf grabs my attention, and I swear the branches on the coastal oaks start to resemble fox heads.

A few moments later, I come upon two women walking uphill. "Heavy breathers coming through!" one jokes. I laugh and step to the side of the trail. Just then, a blur of blue flashes across my peripheral vision. "Oh, my!" I shriek. "Is our breathing that bad?" the woman asks. But they chuckle and continue on before I can explain that I have finally seen an island scrub-jay. Around a corner I spot three more in plain sight. It's as though I have unwittingly passed some initiation and now the birds are revealing

themselves. I'm excited to join what I'm calling the Scrub Club.

I complete the hike and head back toward the pier where I'll catch my return ferry to Ventura. Whales, dolphins, a rare bird and a bonus endemic mouse—it's a successful day even if I didn't see a...

"Fox!" I hear a little girl shout.

By the time I reach a bank of picnic tables across from the pier, a small crowd has formed around an island fox. We all watch in awe as he scavenges for scraps beneath the benches. This sly species sent me on a wild fox chase while he hung out in the very spot where I first stepped foot on the island! And yet, something seems fitting about a creature that exists nowhere else inspiring me to explore a place that's like nowhere else. It's been a successful day, for sure. ●

The rugged Minaret Peaks feed a pretty mountain stream.

STORY AND PHOTOS BY
LONDIE GARCIA PADELSKY

DEVILS POSTPILE

MARVEL AT ONE OF NATURE'S MOST ASTONISHING GEOLOGICAL WONDERS IN THE STUNNING SIERRA NEVADA.

FOR ME, SUMMER OFFICIALLY BEGINS when I hear that the road has opened to Reds Meadow Valley and Devils Postpile National Monument.

It's one of my special wilderness sanctuaries. I've hiked, horse-packed and camped in some of the most pristine backcountry in California's Ansel Adams and John Muir wilderness areas. But when family and friends visit, my favorite place to take them is Devils Postpile.

The road normally opens in mid-June, about the same time that the wildflowers bloom on Minaret Summit. They add a spark of color to spectacular views of the Sierra wilderness and the jagged, snowcapped peaks of the Minaret Pinnacles in the Ritter Range.

The summit is 2 miles past Mammoth Mountain Ski Area, where most day-hiking visitors must board shuttle buses for the 8-mile drive into Reds Meadow Valley. The road is steep, winding and narrow, so the bus offers a leisurely way to sit back and enjoy the scenic pine forests, lush meadows and snowmelt streams.

The Middle Fork of the San Joaquin River—a fisherman's paradise with four species of trout—runs through the valley. Next to the river near the Devils Postpile trailhead are a quaint ranger station, National Park Service offices, picnic tables and the monument's only developed campsites.

Miles of moderate to easy hiking trails wander through Devils Postpile and intersect with both the John Muir and Pacific Crest trails. The Devils Postpile trailhead is a popular destination in the heart of summer, but you'll avoid most of the crowd if you start early in the morning. The mountain air can be a little chilly, but during this quiet time I've spotted black bears, coyotes, marmots, deer and fishermen coexisting peacefully.

It's just a half-mile hike to Devils Postpile, one of the world's finest examples of columnar basalt. This

▼

Rainbow Falls sends up a sun-catching mist as it plunges 101 feet.

POINTS of INTEREST

NOT TO BE MISSED

Take a tour on horseback. Red's Meadow Resort & Pack Station offers 2-hour, 4-hour and all-day guided horseback tours. *redsmeadow.com*

FUN FACT

It is suggested that Devils Postpile formed less than 100,000 years ago when a cooling lava flow cracked into multi-sided columns.

WORDS TO THE WISE

The monument is only open during the summer months. Depending on snow conditions, it usually opens in mid-June.

NEARBY ATTRACTIONS

Yosemite National Park; Mono Lake

geological wonder formed when lava flooded the valley to a depth of 400 feet, then cracked into astonishingly straight, symmetrical columns as it cooled. Glaciation and earthquakes excavated the formation for us to enjoy. A 15-minute side trail leads you to the shimmering glacier-polished tops of the polygonal columns. No matter how many times I visit the Postpile, it's a magnificent sight.

From the Postpile, it's an easy 2-mile hike to Rainbow Falls. But bring water and sunscreen, because the afternoon sun gets intense. The footbridge at Boundary Creek offers a pleasant place to kick off your shoes and cool your feet in the clear, shallow water.

Parts of this path are lush and green, but it also passes through the hauntingly beautiful area left by the fire that burned more than 80% of the monument in 1992. I've photographed lovely patches of lupine growing among charred black tree trunks.

You'll start to hear the thunder of Rainbow Falls when you reach a series of gently descending pumice steps. The scenic overview was placed in exactly the right location for a perfect picture of the highest waterfall on the Middle Fork of the San Joaquin River. And on sunny days, you're almost sure to see a rainbow in the mist.

There's a great spot just past the overview for a picnic. Then, instead of completing the 5-mile loop trail, I usually veer to the right of the sign that points to the Rainbow Falls trailhead. From the falls you hike gradually uphill for a little more than a mile to a horse trail that leads to Red's Meadow Resort & Pack Station. Across the way from the pack station is an outdoorsy general store, a cafe and some small cabins.

This is the valley hub, where you can meet John Muir Trail and Pacific Crest Trail backpackers, day hikers, horse packers, campers and anglers. Whether you've hiked a mile or 100 miles, this is also where you'll want to stop for that well-deserved burger and milk shake to cap off a fantastic day in one of America's most unforgettable places. ●

▼
A cooling lake of lava created Devils Postpile's namesake columns.

STORY BY **DONNA B. ULRICH**
PHOTOS BY **LARRY ULRICH**

SHASTA-TRINITY

FOLLOW A SCENIC BYWAY AND A RUSHING RIVER TO FIND ADVENTURE IN A WILD, WOODED PARADISE.

A BALD EAGLE, perched in a gray pine tree, watches the river below for an afternoon meal. Just upstream, whitewater rafters scream with joy over the thundering rapid called Dynamite. Below, a lone steelhead bides its time, hoping to scale the rapid.

This wild and scenic river, the Trinity, is the lifeblood of Shasta-Trinity National Forest. At 2.2 million acres, it's the largest national forest in California. The Trinity Scenic Byway, state Route 299, the major west-east corridor in Northern California, follows the Trinity River on part of its journey, cutting through the forest's landscapes on its way to and from the coast and inland valleys. Mount Shasta, 100 miles north, dominates the skyline. Along the route you'll find camp-grounds, cabins to rent, rafts to hire, fish to catch, and trails to hike or bike.

Northern California is prone to wildfires. Though devastating, fire is part of the natural cycle. Plants and soil benefit from periodic wildfires and come back healthier and stronger.

My husband, Larry, and I live within a couple of hours of the Trinity River and its surrounding forests, streams and lakes, and we have a cabin in the tiny town of Junction City near the Trinity Alps Wilderness, one of five wilderness areas in the forest and the second-largest wilderness area in the state. The easily accessible lakes, high mountain passes and unusual geology and fauna in this wilderness draw visitors from all over the country.

In summer, we love to visit swimming holes on the river's North Fork. The temperature is almost perfect, and kids love to prove their moxie by swinging out over the deepest parts on a rope.

Occasionally, we hike up Canyon Creek, an icy stream flowing out of the chiseled granite peaks of the Trinity Alps.

Shasta-Trinity National Forest has a long history shaped by gutsy explorers, the 1849 gold rush, logging and salmon. Whether you hike or fish, this wild woodland will captivate you. ●

▼
Wildflowers, including Indian rhubarb, bloom at the McCloud River Preserve.

NOT TO BE MISSED

Shasta Lake is a favorite of both boaters and water-skiers. The lake was created by Shasta Dam, which is more than 600 feet high and ranks as one of the nation's largest concrete structures. And, Shasta Dam Boulevard will lead you to a panoramic view of the region.

Visit Lake Shasta Caverns, a cache of hidden beauty that rivals the area's more conspicuous spots.

Trains that steamed through Dunsmuir along the Southern Pacific Railroad were instrumental in the town's growth, and an old railroading center offers visitors a glimpse of those earlier days. The town is also known for its drinking water.

Cresting at 14,179 feet, Mount Shasta's peak is visible from more than 100 miles away. For a closer look and an eagle's-eye view of the region, follow Everitt Memorial Highway (County Road A10), which climbs nearly halfway to the glacier-clad summit.

The Whiskeytown Lake reservoir is popular for fishing, kayaking, picnicking and windsurfing.

At sunrise, a pastel sky matches the vibrant display of camas lilies in full bloom.

STORY AND PHOTOS BY
LELAND HOWARD

CAMAS PRAIRIE CENTENNIAL MARSH

MOUNTAIN SNOWS AWAKEN THE LANDSCAPE AS SPRING TAKES FLIGHT IN A HAVEN FOR BIRDS.

AS ANOTHER VISITOR and I gazed on vast fields of purple and blue camas lilies in bloom, I smiled. *Well, that should make for some good photographs.*

While south-central Idaho's Camas Prairie Centennial Marsh Wildlife Management Area has a long name, it's also long on beauty.

In a year with much precipitation, these grassy swamps transform into acres of color. The intensity of the lily bloom depends on the level of moisture from snowmelt off of the nearby mountains.

Camas Creek fills with the runoff, then overflows its banks and floods the landscape with standing water between April and June. Typically the flowers peak around mid-June.

From a distance, the rippling fields of flowers have been mistaken for lakes.

Explorer Meriwether Lewis made this error, later writing that what he saw resembled a lake of fine, clear water.

During peak bloom time for the lilies, the 3,100-acre wildlife refuge comes alive with the constant melodious chirps, honks, trills, chitters and warbles from the thousands of waterfowl and shorebirds that migrate here every spring.

The bird-watchers are fun to listen to as they rattle off names like long-billed dowitcher, Wilson's phalarope, lesser yellowlegs, least sandpiper and black-necked stilt.

Gentle breezes make the waist-high blue camas lilies bend and sway, and many of the birds use them for their perches as they go about protecting their territory. Deer and pronghorn antelope are also regularly spotted

▼
Dappled first light reflects on flooded fields.

FUN FACT

The Camas Prairie Centennial marsh is 6,240 acres large.

WORDS TO THE WISE

The area is most popular in late May to early June due to the camas lily bloom. No designated camping is available and there are limited public facilities.

NEARBY ATTRACTION

The Elma Goodman Mountain Bluebird Trail, west of the Camas Prairie on Bennett Mountain Road, is one of the best places to view Idaho's state bird (and other species) when they arrive and nest in spring.

here. Things start to get a lot quieter around mid-July as the waters recede in the summer heat.

The refuge is outside Fairfield, the only city in Camas County. This delightful small town is home to some 400 friendly people, and it plays host to events like Camas Lily Days on the first weekend in June, featuring bloom tours, a celebration of Native American traditions and plenty of activities for families and kids. Be aware that lodging options are less than abundant in Fairfield.

Of course, the remoteness of the region is part of its appeal. Camas is among the least populous of Idaho's 44 counties, and Fairfield residents and visitors alike greatly value seclusion.

In the past, there were a few other towns in the county, and some of their names still show up on maps. One of the routes to the refuge—off U.S. Highway 20—begins where Hill City once stood and passes grain bins and aging buildings.

Learning about the history of the region will help enrich your visit. Blue camas bulbs were a valuable food source for early Native Americans, and a small amount of harvesting still takes place each season.

The bulbs look a little like small potatoes and can be roasted in coals. I have never tasted one, but I hear a bit of salt helps with the flavor. There's also an analogous but toxic species, mountain death camas, so it is important for harvesters to know what they are doing.

There are various historical accounts comparing this idyllic valley and prairie to the Garden of Eden, with an abundance of everything that a person needs to live a good life. And with persuasive prose, a San Francisco newspaper once advertised the landscape as a paradise in just about every way possible.

In 1862, frontiersman Tim Goodale showed emigrants a detour off the Oregon Trail. Known as Goodale's Cutoff, the bypass crossed through the heart of the Camas Prairie. Settlement grew rapidly in the later 1800s, with local population peaking in the early 1900s.

Today, the adjacent lands consist of farms and ranches, with national forests in the higher mountains. Old cabins, grain elevators and schoolhouses provide more historical context and a look back at pioneer days.

This is a high-desert plateau with an average elevation of 5,000 feet, so be advised that some chilly winds can blow even as summer begins in June. My favorite times to visit for taking photos are early morning and late evening, when the subdued light of the sun meeting the horizon is best for observing the rich colors of the blue camas lilies.

But any calm days are splendid for taking your car on the loop drive through the refuge. There is no fee to enter, and there's an official vehicle pullout spot in the center under some large cottonwood trees.

Although the few hiking trails here are not well-defined or well-traveled, it's worth looking for them. They are great for bird-watching, photography or just some leg stretching.

I might get a little gentle ribbing for revealing one of Idaho's hidden gems, but I believe the Camas Prairie is simply too spectacular to keep to myself. ●

▼

A great horned owl patiently perches in a tree.

▼
This fly fisherman casts his line at Basin Lake in the Lemhi Range.

Idaho

STORY AND PHOTOS BY
LELAND HOWARD

LOST RIVER RANGE AND LEMHI MOUNTAIN RANGE

FOLLOW AN IDAHO ADVENTURE LOOP OFF-ROAD TO PLACES OF TRULY UNFORGETTABLE BEAUTY.

STARK. THAT'S HOW some would describe the beauty of the land between Idaho's Lost River Range and Lemhi Mountain Range. Funny, but that word never crossed my mind.

With the tallest mountains in Idaho, the Lost River Range is home to seven peaks topping 12,000 feet, including the state's tallest, Mount Borah. In the summer, hikers, climbers and other adventurers arrive to conquer these summits.

I've spent much of my career as a landscape photographer climbing these rocks, looking for the perfect shot. The best way to explore this area of east-central Idaho is to take what I call the Idaho adventure loop, which follows two historic highways—93 and 28—to scenic wonders.

Exploration of this route requires an adventurous frame of mind and four-wheel drive. The wandering traveler willing to get off the pavement

FUN FACTS

The Lost River Range is made of Proterozoic and Paleozoic sedimentary rocks. The Lost River fault, at the base of the mountains, has been active the last few million years. Large alluvial fans spread out from the steep canyons out over the valley.

The highest point in the Lemhi Mountain Range is Diamond Peak at 12,197 feet. The mid-section of this range was mined for copper, lead, silver and gold in the early 1900s. Evidence can still be found near the Gilmore Summit.

WORDS TO THE WISE

No developed campsites are available at the Lost River Range. The Joe T. Fallini Campground, however, a BLM campground on the Mackay Reservoir, is only a few minutes away from access points and has an incredible view.

▼

This tramway, built in 1917, can be seen in the White Knob Mountains.

will discover small towns with unique character and places so beautiful they escape description.

Arco, a small town with a population of about 880 and the first city in the world to be lit by atomic power, is the start of the adventure tour. Notice the hill with numbers? Each year the senior class paints their graduating year on the rocks. It's a reminder that small-town life is still vibrant. From Arco, take U.S. Highway 93 farther north to Mackay and through the Lost River Valley, where the peaks become increasingly tall and rugged.

Mackay (pronounced "Mackie") is even smaller than Arco but has a rich mining and pioneer history. Some journalists have called this little town the best kept secret in Idaho, citing its western charm, character and proximity to the best hiking and camping in the Lost River Range.

The tour of Mackay's Mine Hill is a must-do. It's self-guided (you can pick up a map at a local restaurant, your lodging or the tourist information center), and the tour covers all of Mackay's mining sites. However, you can drive only up to a certain point. After that, consider hiking, mountain biking or riding an ATV.

North of Mackay, the views of the Lost River are impressive as steep mountains suddenly rise from sagebrush-covered moraines below. The Big Lost River to the west of the highway caps off the views, especially around early October when the valley glows with golden cottonwood trees.

In 1983 these mountains and the valley shifted apart dramatically, about 14 feet in some places, due to a powerful quake that registered 7.3 on the Richter scale. The resulting fault scarp can still be seen on the lower hills below Mount Borah.

Upon reaching the Salmon River, 93 intersects with state Highway 75. Here you'll see lodges between ranch lands, private property, fishing holes and several campgrounds. This section of the wild and scenic Salmon River flows to the northeast from its origins in the Sawtooth Mountains and White Clouds Wilderness Area.

When I'm looking for guaranteed solitude and have plenty of time to just take it slow on dirt roads, I opt for a leisurely detour down Road 11, heading southeast through the tiny towns of May and Patterson (the turn is about one-third of the way to Salmon from the intersection with Highway 75). Not long after Patterson, the road becomes gravel. The views are striking—vast, open sagebrush plains and mighty mountains rising in the distance. But my favorite spot is where the Lost River Range meets the headwaters of the Pahsimeroi River, a tributary to the Salmon River.

Back on 93, the rustic town of Salmon lies at the northern tip of the Lemhi Range, which runs along the east side of the adventure loop. Salmon's origins include mining, lumber and family ranching. Time passes and cultures change. Now a visitor will find art galleries along with fishing, rafting, hunting and adventure guides. Numerous restaurants and lodging opportunities are available; however, I can say that this town still certainly deserves the "rustic" designation.

Perhaps its biggest claim to fame is the Sacajawea Interpretive, Cultural and Educational Center. Sacajawea, who helped explorers Lewis and Clark on their expedition to the Pacific Ocean, was born in the Lemhi Valley, and the park is an impressive tribute. It's open year-round, and the gardens and trails throughout the 71-acre park make it a worthwhile detour.

▼

The Lost River Range glows at sunrise.

Indian paintbrush and other wildflowers carpet a ridge in the Beaverhead Mountains.

▼

In Salmon, a bronze statue of Sacajawea is a reminder of her role in Lewis and Clark's expedition.

A bronze sculpture of Sacajawea standing with mountains in the background is an admirable accolade to a remarkable woman.

Back on the adventure loop, head southeast on state Highway 28 as it climbs toward Gilmore Summit. Gilmore is a fascinating ghost town situated on the pass just a couple of miles to the west of the highway. Drive from Gilmore Summit and see vast views of public land. Water from the mountains on both sides collects in the valley to form Birch Creek.

More canyons invite exploration, and a good route with historical interest isn't far south from the pass. A dirt road takes you west to the Birch Creek Charcoal Kilns Interpretive Site, which has century-old beehive-shaped kilns built to produce charcoal for nearby mines. The kilns are to the north of Diamond Peak, which, at 12,197 feet, is the highest in the Lemhi Range. This peak is about 35 miles from Mount Borah. There are many easy pullouts farther south along Birch Creek where campers can fish waters with mountain views.

Taking state Highway 33 west leads back to Arco, the starting point of our journey. To get the most out of a trip to this area, take your time. Unwind, enjoy the silence of these natural landscapes, and watch the sun rise and set over high mountain peaks. ●

▼
Alpenglow graces the rugged face of McGown Peak.

Idaho

STORY AND PHOTOS BY
LELAND HOWARD

SAWTOOTH MOUNTAINS

TRAILS LEADING TO JAGGED PEAKS, HIDDEN LAKES AND
MEADOWS LUSH WITH WILDFLOWERS DELIVER MOUNTAIN
DRAMA AT ITS BEST.

TRAVELING NORTH past the Idaho resort towns of Ketchum and Sun Valley, it's easy to think the views can't get any better as you pass under the Boulder Mountains on the way to Galena Summit. The Boulders are spectacular in their own right, but just over the pass a traveler finds an extraordinary view of crags and ridges that inspired the name Sawtooth Range.

Officially called the Sawtooth National Recreation Area, this preserve consists of four mountain ranges with more than 50 peaks over 10,000 feet, and the rugged Sawtooth Wilderness as the main attraction. I've been taking photographs for a living for more than 30 years, and I try to make at least one trip a year to this amazing place. I've hiked and backpacked along many trails through the mountains. There are so many pristine mountain lakes that some don't even have names. Waterfalls and soaring peaks beg you to stop and stare.

The Sawtooth Valley is a high mountain plateau, and in some years there will still be patches of snow left on the pass in late May or early June. Spring usually begins in mid-June, with wildflowers blooming in the meadows. The autumn color can start as early as September; some of my favorite trips have been in the fall. Aspen forests mix with the pines, and some of the leaves turn red instead of the usual aspen yellow. I've heard that minerals in the soil cause the striking hue, but whatever the reason, it's like icing on the cake to see such bright colors under the jagged peaks.

Oh, and by the way, the White Cloud Mountains are to the east on the other side of the road—another mountain range with a fitting name. It's remarkable that this range—with many peaks over 10,000 feet, and the highest of them all, Castle Peak, at about 11,800 feet—remains little known. This unbelievably pristine region, with

NOT TO BE MISSED
Saddle up and venture into this majestic wilderness on horseback. Several outfitters operate in the Sawtooths. Visit *stanleycc.org* to learn more.

FUN FACT
Few have ever seen a wolverine because they avoid humans and prefer remote forest areas and high-mountain cirques. However, track verifications and sightings confirm that a great number of them inhabit Idaho's central mountain ranges, including the Sawtooths.

WORDS TO THE WISE
Wildflower lovers should visit in early summer, when the slopes are abloom with lupines, scarlet gilias, fireweeds, bluebells and columbines. Miles of trails thread through the forests of firs, pines and aspens, and crystal-clear streams and rivers lace the area.

If you decide to stay, the visitor center is a valuable resource. When exploring, look for mountain goats, pronghorns, bighorn sheep and elk.

▼
Hell Roaring Lake looks like glass as mist lingers over it.

its abundant mountain lakes, has been designated a national wilderness area.

For the perfect sunrise view in the Sawtooths, go through the town of Stanley and take the turn to Stanley Lake. The water reflects the sharp pinnacle of McGown Peak, and everything lines up perfectly for the first rays of light. This is also a good place to see meadows carpeted with wildflowers; just follow the trail from the campground. Speaking of trails, they're abundant, and many can be used for a nice day hike that leads to mountain lakes and waterfalls. It's hard to pick a favorite, but I often find myself taking the Iron Creek Trail on the north end of the range. It's less traveled than many, and after only about an hour you find yourself standing on the shores of a lake surrounded by mountain peaks.

Unlike some places I've explored in the West, the Sawtooths don't require that you backpack to have the trip of a lifetime. There are a variety of guest ranches, some catering to large groups like family reunions or weddings. Some really are world class, and if you want to create your own adventure—whether it involves hiking, horseback riding, mountain biking, fishing, whitewater rafting or even swimming in natural hot springs—they can help. Of course, you can also take advantage of local guides and tours. The Stanley Chamber of Commerce website, *stanleycc.org*, is a good place to start.

Ernest Hemingway lived in Sun Valley and loved the Sawtooth Wilderness and the surrounding landscapes. I'm confident you'll see why. This place in central Idaho is special, to say the least. ●

Goat Lake sits in a steep glacial cirque surrounded by cliffs. The trail is rugged, making the lake a remote destination.

The day's first light sets the Fire Wave all aglow.

STORY AND PHOTOS BY
DENNIS FRATES

VALLEY OF FIRE

EXPLORE AN OTHERWORLDLY LANDSCAPE DOTTED WITH MIGHTY ROCK FORMATIONS AND SIGNS OF THE ANCIENTS.

AS SOON AS I ENTERED Nevada's Valley of Fire State Park, I realized that the travel guides hadn't done justice to this magnificent location just a simple day trip from Las Vegas.

The park, about 65 miles from Las Vegas in the Mojave Desert, encompasses 40,000 acres of some of the most stunning rock formations I have found in the deserts of the Southwest. Vibrant red Aztec sandstone formations with names like Elephant Rock, Rainbow Vista and Beehives dot the horizon. Time and the powers of nature (water and wind) created this surreal landscape set against an often brilliant blue sky.

Established in 1935, Valley of Fire is Nevada's first state park. The name is attributed to an AAA official who, in the 1920s, was traveling through the area on a road built to connect Salt Lake City and Los Angeles. As the sun set, he noted that the sky's red glow made the entire valley seem to be ablaze.

Though the park's proximity to Las Vegas makes it popular for weddings and day trips, Valley of Fire isn't crowded. You can always find a serene trail to trek or a spot to yourself.

Getting your bearings will help you enjoy Valley of Fire, and the best place to do that is the visitor center. Browse the exhibits to learn about the park's geography, wildlife and history before venturing out. Rangers can direct you to that perfect hike or vista.

The park has something to offer everyone. If you like to lace up your sneakers or boots and explore on foot, follow one of the 12 designated trails in the park. Most offer short and easy hikes (about a mile round trip) with wonders waiting around every corner. No matter what direction you look, you'll see spectacular stone marvels and incredible splashes of color.

POINTS of INTEREST

FUN FACT

The World Atlatl Association hosts a spear-throwing competition every spring in Valley of Fire State Park. *parks.nv.gov/parks/valley-of-fire*

NEARBY ATTRACTIONS

Northward toward Overton, the Lost City Museum holds remnants of the long-vanished Anasazi civilization that flourished in the region until A.D. 1200.

To the southeast is Lake Mead National Recreation Area and the Hoover Dam that created this 110-mile-long lake. It's a mecca for swimmers, boaters, windsurfers, divers, anglers and sightseers.

To the southwest just past Las Vegas (also nearby), Red Rock Canyon National Conservation Area has a 13-mile, one-way, horseshoe-shaped drive that takes visitors past spectacular sandstone cliffs and towering peaks. Turnouts along the way lead to stunning vistas and inviting trails, such as the short hikes to Lost Creek and Pine Creek Canyon.

▼

The view from Fire Cave (aka Windstone Arch) shows diverse geology.

If scenic drives are your passion, you'll enjoy a cruise along Valley of Fire Highway. This 7-mile drive winds through the heart of the park and takes you past rock formations including Elephant Rock (so named because it's shaped like one) and Seven Sisters.

Starting from the west, take a slight detour along a 3-mile scenic loop road to reach Arch Rock, a fragile stone arc created by centuries of erosion (and a fantastic photo opportunity), and Atlatl Rock, known for petroglyphs. Nearby, Petrified Logs is an off-road area featuring petrified wood left behind by an ancient sea.

The main road winds past other fascinating stones, including Piano Rock and the Beehives, a collection of mounds dramatically carved by wind and water to resemble a beehive. A short trail will take you up close and around them.

Another drive, Mouse's Tank Road (also called White Domes Road for a collection of cream-colored sandstone mounds), heads north toward Mouse's Tank Trail. There you'll find the greatest concentration of petroglyphs in Nevada. Human history in the Moapa Valley goes back thousands of years, and when Pueblo and Paiute Indians made seasonal camps here, they portrayed their lives in vivid petroglyphs, many along a spot known as Petroglyph Canyon.

You'll want to get out of the car and take a short 1-mile hike (there and back) to explore the Fire Wave's vibrant ribbons of red sandstone, quite similar to the Wave in Page, Arizona. Rainbow Vista offers a panoramic view of multicolored rocks dating back to the days of the dinosaurs.

The best time to hike the park's many colorful hills and canyons is spring and autumn. Summers can be blisteringly hot and uncomfortable. This is the Mojave Desert, with only about 4 inches of rainfall annually and a light dusting of snow in the winter.

Most of the many animals native to the area are nocturnal. If you hike very early or late in the day, you are more likely to see some of the critters that inhabit the park, including coyote, bobcat, kit fox, skunk, antelope and bighorn sheep.

I've photographed deserts all over the Southwest, but Valley of Fire State Park keeps calling me back to search for yet another hidden gem. A ranger once told me there were many arches in the park still waiting to be discovered, and I find something new every time I visit. ❧

Every curve and ◀ bend leads to wonder in the Valley of Fire.

Kokanee salmon, a favorite among anglers, spawn in the Wallowa River.

STORY AND PHOTOS BY
DAVID JENSEN

WALLOWA LAKE

VENTURE TO A LAND WHERE CLEAR WATERS AND MIGHTY MOUNTAINTOPS BECKON EXPLORERS.

EMINENTLY QUOTABLE on so many subjects, Chief Joseph, a leader of the Nez Perce Indians, once said that he loved the Wallowa Valley of Oregon "more than all the rest of the world." Visit Wallowa Lake State Park and you will understand why.

Here, dramatic mountains soar into the sky and stand abruptly over a picturesque valley. Sculpted into classic alpine shapes by massive glaciers during the last ice age, these peaks gleam with snow late into the summer. Then it gets better. A 4-mile-long lake lies precisely where the Wallowa Mountains meet the valley, a ribbon of crystal clear water impounded by spectacular glacial moraines.

Wallowa Lake State Park, a haven in the state's far northeast corner, sits at

the gateway to the Wallowa Mountains. Though promoted as the "Switzerland of America" for nearly a century, this area has long been protected from the crush of crowds because it is one of Oregon's most remote destinations.

The park itself covers about 200 acres situated among ponderosa pines on the lake's south shore. Despite its 4,400-foot elevation and snowy winters that often freeze the lake, the park is open year-round and is an ideal base for exploring the mountains. Its campground has plenty of amenities and accommodates both tent campers and folks in RVs.

Just outside the park is the trailhead to the Eagle Cap Wilderness—quick access to 500 miles of trails for day hiking, horseback riding, mountain climbing, or multiday expeditions

WORDS TO THE WISE

The Wallowa Lake Marina is located within the park and is open seasonally. It offers moorage rentals and various watercraft for rent. *wallowalakemarina.com*

There is year-round camping, but it's advisable to make your reservations 6 months in advance. *oregonstateparks.reserveamerica.com*

NEARBY ATTRACTIONS

Check out Hat Point Overlook, 54 miles to the northeast, which provides views of Hells Canyon, the deepest gorge in North America.

Joseph Canyon Viewpoint is 42 miles north of Wallowa Lake State Park.

Just north of the park are Iwetemlaykin State Heritage Site and Nez Perce National Historical Park, marking the ancestral homeland of the Nez Perce. *stateparks.oregon.gov*

▼

Six Mile Meadow is a popular stop along the way to Lakes Basin.

into the backcountry. If your time is limited, walk less than a mile to the area known as Boy Scout Falls on the west fork of the Wallowa River. Or, if you are an experienced hiker with a day to explore, climb Chief Joseph Mountain, a steep vertical ascent of more than 5,000 feet that leads to dizzying views of the lake and the bucolic valley below.

If you prefer exploring the area without too much exertion, the Wallowa Lake Tramway is only a five-minute walk from the campground. The cable gondola will carry you effortlessly to the top of Mount Howard, over 8,000 feet high. There

you can dine at the Summit Grill, Oregon's highest restaurant, while taking in sweeping views of mountains and canyons.

The tramway makes it so easy to get there you might be tempted to climb higher and continue on foot along an unofficial trail to the 9,380-foot summit of East Peak for even more incredible vistas of the craggy peaks in Oregon's largest wilderness area.

Back at the state park, water sports beckon—swimming, water skiing, canoeing, kayaking and fishing. You can rent just about every kind of watercraft at the marina, including paddleboards and pontoon boats.

Of special interest to anglers are kokanee, landlocked freshwater sockeye salmon. Every September the kokanee turn a brilliant red and spawn in the braided stream entering the lake. Fishing licenses and gear, including tackle and bait, are available from the boat rental concessionaire at the Wallowa Lake Marina.

Historic Wallowa Lake Lodge is just a three-minute walk from your campsite. Built in 1923 in the style of classic national park lodges and with an elegant dining room, it was featured prominently in the PBS series *Great Lodges of the National Parks.*

You'll find other restaurants, rental cabins and gift shops nearby. Or drive 6 miles north along the lakeshore to the tourist town of Joseph, which has many restaurants, nice art galleries and a great museum. Don't miss the wonderful natural history center called Wallowology (don't even try pronouncing that), which is staffed by naturalists who are passionate about the science of the lake and the surrounding mountains.

The Nez Perce called these lands home until 1877, when the U.S. Army forced them into exile. During your wanderings through the lake, visit the sacred ancestral places of the tribe, such as the Old Chief Joseph Gravesite in the Nez Perce National Historical Park and the adjacent Iwetemlaykin State Heritage Site.

Iwetemlaykin means "at the edge of the lake" in the Nez Perce language. A peaceful place where you might spot deer, fox and raptors as well as views of the Wallowa Mountains along a mile-long hiking trail, this site was added to the park in 2009 after a long campaign by the tribe. Actively engaged in managing and conserving the ecology of the Wallowa Lake basin, the Nez Perce remain deeply connected to this special place. ▪

▼

Boy Scout Falls is a hiker's delight.

A gentle rain falls on the Burr Trail in Long Canyon.

STORY AND PHOTOS BY
LAURENCE PARENT

GRAND STAIRCASE–ESCALANTE

BEAUTY AND AMAZEMENT ABOUND IN THE COUNTRY'S LARGEST
NATIONAL MONUMENT.

ON THE FIRST MORNING of my journey, I take state Route 12 east from the Utah town of Escalante. The road soon enters the Grand Staircase-Escalante National Monument, at 1.9 million acres the largest national monument in the United States. About the size of the state of Delaware, it's neighbored by Bryce Canyon and Capitol Reef national parks as well as state parks and other recreation areas. The Grand Staircase gets its name from a series of plateaus that descend from Bryce Canyon.

At first, the dry terrain around me is flat and dotted with juniper trees. That changes abruptly when I crest the rim of the Escalante River Canyon.

Red-and-white sandstone cliffs and bluffs fall away from the roadside in great swooping curves. Millions of years ago, ancient sand dunes solidified into these massive layers of stone that are once again being carved back into sand by water and wind.

I slow and wind my way down into the canyon, stopping at the trailhead at the bottom to admire the red rock walls towering above me. The river slides by under a highway bridge, shaded by arching green cottonwoods. The trail along the river tempts me, but I continue a short distance up the highway to Calf Creek Campground. There I pull on a day pack and hike up

POINTS of INTEREST

FUN FACT

The difference between a hoodoo and a pinnacle, or spire, is that hoodoos have a variable thickness, with a shape similar to a totem pole. A spire, on the other hand, has a smoother profile or uniform thickness that tapers from the ground upward.

WORDS TO THE WISE

This monument is one of the most remote regions of the American Southwest. The area is a favorite among locals, but bring plenty of water, provisions and a current weather forecast if you venture into the district—untimely changes in the weather, including snow and flash floods, can be life-threatening and sometimes close the road—always come prepared for a long, cold stay.

NEARBY ATTRACTIONS

Bryce Canyon National Park; Capitol Reef National Park; Dixie National Forest; Escalante Petrified Forest State Park; Zion National Park

▼

Spanning about 100 feet, Phipps Arch offers a feeling of awe.

the deep canyon along the clear waters of Calf Creek. I take a few moments to stop and admire Native American petroglyphs.

In 3 easy miles, the canyon narrows, and I hear roaring water before arriving at an amphitheater walled with Navajo sandstone, where a 126-foot waterfall pours down into a deep plunge pool. Finding this idyllic oasis in the desert surprises me. Calf Creek Falls was so named because its shape made it a natural pen for cattle in the late 1800s.

The next morning I drive the road to Burr Trail. Past imposing ridges of white slickrock, across the tree-lined waters of Deer Creek, the road drops into the red rock passage of Long Canyon. It follows the creek

downstream for several miles until abruptly popping out onto a high point with views of the distant Circle Cliffs.

I continue through high desert country, finally stopping where the pavement ends at the boundary with Capitol Reef National Park, then head back toward Escalante. Just short of town I turn south onto Hole-in-the-Rock Road, named for a rock crevice at its southeast end. There, in 1880, a Mormon expedition blasted and carved a precipitous crack in the 1,200-foot cliffs that line Glen Canyon to allow 83 wagons, 250 people, and more than 1,000 head of livestock to pass through.

Although the Kaiparowits Plateau looms in the west, the washboard road passes through mostly flat desert dotted with sagebrush for its 55 long miles. I have to work a little to find interesting places along this dusty route—until I turn off the road for a short side trip to Devil's Garden. There I wander for an hour through a small maze of sandstone ridges, hoodoos and arches as the evening light turns golden, painting the rock with brilliant color.

The next morning I drive back down Hole-in-the-Rock Road, hoping for more surprises. A short side road leads to a bleak parking area above the Dry Fork of Coyote Gulch. I follow a trail that drops quickly down into the bottom of the gulch, walk downstream and scramble up into a side canyon named Peek-a-boo Gulch.

Small arches and scalloped sandstone walls in the slot draw me upstream until the canyon widens. Then I hike a half-mile and drop into the aptly named Spooky Gulch. The slot becomes so narrow that I have to turn sideways in some places to get through. Much of the time, the sky above isn't even visible, and the light is murky and dim.

Slot canyons are addictive, so I drive back up the road to an unmarked parking lot looking for more of them. The terrain is impressive as I walk east, descending into another canyon that joins broad Harris Wash, and spot the narrow Zebra Canyon slot disappearing into a cliff face.

As I enter this canyon known for its striped walls, I wade through a pool and remember the danger of flash floods. Gushing waters can sweep through these narrow canyons without warning. Still, the beauty is irresistible, and I take many photographs of the undulating walls as I snake into the depths of the canyon.

Looking at these magnificent surroundings, I realize I have touched only a tiny fraction of the monument. It would be a lifelong adventure to see all of its beautiful places. ●

▼
Rock layers give Zebra Canyon its stripes.

Artist Ridge Trail offers this stunning view of Mount Baker.

STORY BY **MARY LIZ AUSTIN**
PHOTOS BY **TERRY DONNELLY**

MOUNT BAKER-SNOQUALMIE

ONE OF THE WORLD'S MOST PICTURESQUE MOUNTAINS IS JUST THE APPETIZER IN THIS NORTHWEST FEAST FOR THE SENSES.

VISITING THE NORTHWEST is like reading a menu from a five-star restaurant: How do you choose from all the amazing delicacies? Do you pick the classic drive to Mount Rainier, or order a delightful tour of the San Juan Islands? Perhaps the sampler platter—an all-encompassing excursion to Olympic National Park? This time we chose an often overlooked, slightly out-of-the-way drive through Austin Pass up to Artist Point, in the heart of the soul-satisfying Mount Baker-Snoqualmie National Forest.

From Bellingham on the coast, head east on state Route 542, and 58 miles later you'll reach the top of Austin Pass. As you crest the ridgeline at mile 55, the reflection of Mount Shuksan in Picture Lake will be your first tasty bite. This view, one of the most beautiful Washington state has to offer, has actually been used on a brochure advertising the Swiss Alps! Mount Shuksan is said to be the world's most photographed mountain.

It's a good place to stop for a hike. The easy trail wraps around the lake, and strategically placed resting spots mark the best places to drink in the delectable scenery. This road remains open year-round for travelers to the nearby Mount Baker Ski Area, a major commercial ski complex. It's known for having some of the deepest snow anywhere in North America, with an average annual snowfall of 647 inches, or 54 feet.

Save your lunch for the Heather Meadow picnic area, just a mile farther on, where you can also take in the amazing views of the North Cascades. Afterward, stretch your legs and cleanse your palate in the web of short trails winding down the hillside to a small creek. Here the path crosses

POINTS of INTEREST

NOT TO BE MISSED

Go rafting and ride the beautiful glacier-fed Nooksack River on family-friendly raft tours with spectacular views of Mount Baker. *riverrider.com*

SIDE TRIPS

At the town of Concrete head north to 9-mile-long Baker Lake. A recreational reservoir east of snowcapped Mount Baker—a 10,781-foot volcano that on occasion still spews out clouds of steam—the lake is a popular place for hiking, canoeing and angling for trout and sockeye salmon.

Jagged and forbidding, 5,979-foot Mount Index is graced by high waterfalls. In the mountain's shadow, the turbulent Skykomish River (known locally as "the Sky") poses challenges to whitewater rafters and invites anglers casting for salmon and steelhead. In the timbered foothills outside the town of Gold Bar lies Wallace Falls State Park. A trail here winds to a 265-foot waterfall, rewarding hikers with pretty views.

▼

Mount Shuksan is reflected in the aptly named Picture Lake.

a charming stonework bridge and continues along the shoreline of sparkling Upper Bagley Lake.

Back on the highway, the last 2 miles jaunt upward through Austin Pass and end at the aptly named Artist Point, with its truly inspiring panorama. This may be the most scenic parking lot in the Northwest. At the north end, there's a bird's-eye view of the Bagley Lakes area. The south end faces the striking snowcapped peak of Mount Baker, one of the highest points in the state.

To the east, a fairly flat walking trail follows the ridgeline paralleling Mount Baker, providing spectacular views that challenge you to decide where to look first. Look to your right and see Mount Baker's sparkling white glaciers. Look to your left, and an incline introduces an intimate

view of Mount Shuksan. Spread out below, summer meltwater from the glaciers forms small tarns, or pools, that reflect views of Shuksan back up to our eager eyes.

Summer also means wildflowers. Green sedges and pink-blossomed fireweed and spirea edge the shoreline of Picture Lake, while mountain heather dots the high alpine slopes. For me, early October is when the flavors of the scenery truly come together. Warm hues of mountain ash, huckleberry and meadow grass against the muted blue autumn sky simply take my breath away.

After an afternoon of feasting my eyes on the expansive views of Austin Pass, I'm full to bursting. I don't think I could take in another craggy slope or vivid reflection. Well, maybe just one more peek. ◗

▼
Huckleberry and mountain ash splash a hillside along Bagley Creek with sumptuous fall color.

▼
The waters at West Tensleep Lake invite kayakers and fishermen to frolic.

STORY BY
KEN KEFFER

BIGHORN MOUNTAINS

DISCOVER THE BEST TRAILS, FISHING HOLES AND SCENIC
DRIVES IN THIS SPECIAL WYOMING SPOT.

IT'S HARD TO IMAGINE an entire mountain range can be underappreciated, but that's the case for the Bighorns.

Impossible to miss on a trip from the Black Hills to Yellowstone, the 100-mile-long and 60-mile-wide range is a prominent feature in north central Wyoming. Countless travelers think of the Bighorns as an obstacle, not a destination. Yet from the basins to the peaks, the range provides a cross section of natural history and fun outdoor recreation.

Situated at the eastern base of the Bighorn Mountains, the town of Buffalo has been base camp for many of my adventures. As a Wyoming native, I'll always claim the town as my home. I go back to Wyoming every year to see my family—and my mountains. With exceptions during Longmire Days and fair week, the Johnson County seat is a quiet home for about 4,600 people. I always expect to run into someone I know at the Dash Inn, the locally owned fast(ish) food place.

Across the road from the eatery is the eastern terminus of Clear Creek Trail. Heading upstream along the cottonwood-lined banks of its namesake body of water, this paved path offers up mountain views the entire way. From town, many trailheads provide easy access to the entire path.

The section near the Veterans' Home of Wyoming is especially scenic. And you can see history along the trail, including a steel pony truss railroad bridge from the 1880s and an abandoned hydroelectric power plant from 1914. Though the latter site is covered in graffiti, the castlelike architecture style is impressive.

Crazy Woman Square, in the heart of downtown Buffalo, is situated right along the Clear Creek Trail. This small park was formerly home to

NOT TO BE MISSED

A local favorite, the scenic drive through Crazy Woman Canyon follows the course of a creek as it winds through the canyon. Closed seasonally, the road navigates rocky terrain, so high-clearance vehicles are recommended.

Between Buffalo and Sheridan, Fort Phil Kearny was established in 1866 to protect travelers along the Bozeman Trail. Learn about fort life and the colorful characters who sought refuge there. *fortphilkearny.com*

The James T. Saban Fire Lookout Tower, named to honor a Forest Service ranger who perished in the 1937 Blackwater Fire, is a fire platform, no longer in service, at the end of a hike.

The Medicine Lodge State Archaeological Site, a 750-foot-long cliff face, is known for hundreds of prehistoric petroglyphs and pictographs.

Northern Bighorn sites include Sibley Lake, Shell Falls and the Medicine Wheel National Historic Landmark. *travelwyoming.com*

▼

Wildlife, including bull elk, roam freely in the forest.

a Ben Franklin store, lost to arson years ago.

Between the square and the courthouse, the historic Occidental Hotel remains an area icon. Built in the 1880s, the hotel and saloon has seen visitors from Teddy Roosevelt to Calamity Jane.

If you find yourself in Buffalo on a Thursday night, take in the jam session in the hotel lobby. Local musicians carry the night, but it's always fun to have visitors sitting in on some tunes.

Next door to the courthouse is the Jim Gatchell Memorial Museum, which houses artifacts of frontier life including firearms, clothing, photographs and wagons. Childhood visits filled my head with visions of life on the edge of civilization. Glowing under a black light, the display of gemstones, rocks, and, if memory serves me, a horse tooth, has stuck with me over the decades.

The idea that early settlers made a living off the land, surviving by hunting and fishing, awed me. I was one of many Keffer family grandchildren who learned fly-fishing on stunted brook trout in cold Bighorn Mountain streams. Our favorite fishing holes included North Clear Creek near Hunter Ranger Station and the beaver ponds along Sourdough Creek.

According to Grandpa, fishing was slow on days we weren't "holding our mouths right." But one memorable Fourth of July picnic at Meadowlark Lake, the fishing was hot, even though the temperatures weren't. My cousin and I were paddling an inflatable raft when the biggest, fluffiest, wettest snowflakes started falling from the sky.

Our relatives retreated to their vehicles; however, since the fish were biting, we hearty anglers continued thrashing the waters. Grandpa was proud of our dedication, but Grandma thought we were knuckleheads.

Be sure to have your camera ready at Burgess Overlook, one of many scenic vistas in Bighorn National Forest.

▼
Crazy Woman Creek flows through a canyon of the same name. No one knows for sure who inspired the name.

▼

Medicine Wheel National Historic Landmark is a sacred place for many Native Americans.

The July snow didn't stick, but if you're in town when it does, head right across the highway to Willow Park. Groomed trails are ideal for cross-country skiing throughout the winter. Snowshoeing is also an option all over the Bighorns.

Not far from Meadowlark Lake is West Tensleep Lake, with many daytrip options, including to West Tensleep Falls or along Middle Tensleep Trail. You can access the Cloud Peak Wilderness area from the popular West Tensleep Trailhead.

The scenic Cloud Peak Skyway traverses the Bighorn Mountains, linking Buffalo to the town of Ten Sleep. The storied byway is named for the highest peak in the range, which touches the sky at 13,166 feet. The swath of highway travels along stands of lodgepole pine forest dotted with mountain meadows. Look for moose, elk and mule deer grazing these fields.

The landscape takes on a much drier feel as U.S. Highway 16 winds through Tensleep Canyon, where rock climbers are drawn to the rugged canyon walls found there. As you continue west down the mountain toward Ten Sleep, give your vehicle's brakes a rest and take in the stunning views from roadside pullouts. Soon you'll leave the mountains behind and enter the arid Bighorn Basin.

The Bighorn Mountains are more than just the most scenic obstacle on the way to Yellowstone. While my kinfolk want to keep this area a secret, once you get there, they will welcome you with a nod of the hat, a friendly smile and plenty of advice on places to explore. ●

▼

Lake Helen is nestled snuggly in the Bighorn Mountains of Wyoming.

" Beauty of whatever kind, in its supreme development, invariably excites the sensitive soul to tears."

—EDGAR ALLAN POE

SOUTHWEST

VERDE VALLEY

ORGAN PIPE CACTUS

CHIRICAHUA

NORTHERN RIO GRANDE

PALO DURO CANYON

Big Balanced Rock sits upon a small perch.

STORY AND PHOTOS BY
LAURENCE PARENT

CHIRICAHUA

WITH NAMES LIKE OLD MAID, SEA CAPTAIN AND DUCK ON A ROCK, THE FORMATIONS IN THIS LANDSCAPE ARE A MUST-SEE.

THE MOUNTAINS RISE in the distance as I drive across Arizona's grassy Sulphur Springs Valley to the entrance of Chiricahua National Monument. My anticipation builds as I enter the park, because this is a homecoming of sorts. I lived here when my father was a park ranger, and I have fond memories of it.

Bonita Canyon Drive is an 8-mile scenic route through the park. The road narrows as I follow it upstream past the visitor center. Oaks, pines and Arizona cypresses cloak the canyon bottom. Rock pinnacles rise from the canyon walls, towering over the road. The Apache called this area "the land of standing-up rocks" for a reason.

The pinnacles got their start about 27 million years ago when the massive Turkey Creek Volcano spewed a thick layer of ash over 1,200 square miles. These superheated particles melted together when they fell, forming rhyolite rock. Millions of years of uplift, fracturing and erosion created the forest of pinnacles that rise up today.

Many of the formations are named for their distinctive shapes. The Sea Captain and the China Boy loom above me as I drive steadily up the canyon. The road climbs a high ridge and ends at Massai Point, a popular picnic spot with 360-degree views of the surrounding Chiricahua Mountains.

With their diverse climate, the Chiricahuas are home to a variety of animal species. The weather at the

NOT TO BE MISSED

Spot the birds! Look for hundreds of species of birds during Wings Over Willcox, an annual birding festival.

FUN FACTS

For centuries this area was part of the Chiricahua Apache traditional homeland.

The range in altitude here, from about 5,000 to more than 7,000 feet, helps to create a hospitable environment for a wide assortment of plants.

The monument has 17 miles of hiking trails, a campground and picnic areas. Of historic interest is the Faraway Ranch, a pioneer homestead that was a working cattle and guest ranch. From here a paved 6-mile scenic drive leads through a maze of canyons to Massai Point, which offers views of the surrounding valleys and has an exhibit building with displays describing the region's very dramatic geology.

WORDS TO THE WISE

The site is open year-round. *nps.gov/chir*

▼

Visit Echo Canyon at sunset for an amazing view.

base of the mountains is drastically different from that on the peaks.

I pull on my pack and start hiking a 9-mile loop down the Echo Canyon Trail. I follow it out on a ridge, making my way through the towering rocks. Soon the trail winds down into Echo Canyon, squeezing through narrow slots in the stone walls.

I follow the route into Rhyolite Canyon and then up the Sarah Deming Trail to Heart of Rocks. The mountain-top area is well-named: It's a true ground zero for pinnacles and rock formations of every size and shape.

Big Balanced Rock, a massive boulder somehow perched on a ridiculously small base, amazes me. I wander the loop that snakes through the rocky

wonderland, smiling at Punch and Judy, Duck on a Rock and Old Maid. Hardy pines, oaks and junipers grow out of cracks and small drainages. I scramble onto a high point and admire the sea of pinnacles surrounding me. The shadows lengthen as the sun slides low into the western sky, outlining every rock with golden light.

The sinking sun makes me realize that it's time for me to hike back to my car at Massai Point. I know it will be dark by the time I reach my vehicle, but I have a headlamp to light my way. Watching the sun set over Heart of Rocks makes the late hike worthwhile. This place is every bit as good as I remembered. I'll be back with my own kids. ❧

There are curving rock grottos to explore.

The organ pipe cactus is an astonishing plant species with its many arms, large stature and long lifespan.

STORY BY **MARY LIZ AUSTIN**

ORGAN PIPE CACTUS

SHARE THE STARK SPLENDOR OF AN EXOTIC DESERT WORLD— AND SOME MIGHTY TASTY COWBOY COFFEE.

MY HUSBAND, TERRY, AND I have been driving for three days, straight south from the Pacific Northwest. We love snow, but it's time to search for signs of spring and feel the sun on our faces.

Our destination is the remote Organ Pipe Cactus National Monument, a gem tucked away in southern Arizona's vast Sonoran Desert. Thanks to its unique crossroads locale, the monument is home to a wide range of specialized plants and animals, including its namesake cactus.

The organ pipe cactus is a rare species in the U.S., and this stretch of desert marks its northern range. With their multiple stems, the cactuses resemble old pipe organs, and with a little imagination you can almost hear them serenading the desert.

An organ pipe cactus can have up to 100 arms, reach 25 feet in height and live for a century. These cactuses bloom from May through June with 3-inch flowers that are pollinated at night by bats and moths.

We search for photo locations as soon as we arrive, because it usually takes a few days of persistent scouting to locate the best spots and capture them with the best lighting conditions.

Driving down state Route 85, the main road into the national monument, we begin to see swaths of blooming brittlebush. It's thrilling to see these 4-foot-tall shrubs covered with bright yellow blossoms.

We pull into a tight sandy turnout and hike out into the desert in search of good flowering specimens and dramatic views. Soon we lose sight of our truck and are absorbed in the beauty of the spring desert. I'm lost in thought when a gruff voice snaps me out of my reverie.

A patrolling park ranger has noticed our truck squeezed into its spot, which is apparently an unauthorized pullout. We're a stone's throw from the Mexican border, and he wonders what we're doing here. After we assure him that we're searching for wildflowers, not

NOT TO BE MISSED

Ajo Mountain Drive, a 21-mile loop, winds through the monument, offering scenic views and picnic areas. The park has several hiking trails, some through the desert and others into the Ajo Mountains.

FUN FACTS

The organ pipe cactus has an egg-shaped red fruit that matures in July, splitting open as it ripens to disclose black seeds that are consumed by many of the hundreds of species of birds observed in this area. Fruit that drops to the ground provides food for many types of animals. The park's 500 square miles of desert is the northernmost habitat of this rare plant.

WORDS TO THE WISE

The site is open year-round except on Christmas. *nps.gov/orpi*

▼
Saguaro and cholla cactuses catch the sun's rays in the Ajo Mountains.

people, he warms up considerably. We talk about the park, his job and our travels. Before he leaves, our new friend, Ranger Steve, invites us to his house in the morning for some cowboy coffee.

Still, we decide to stick to the main roads after that. State Route 85 cuts through the monument from north to south. From the visitor center you can take two drives; they are both unpaved but well graded.

The Puerto Blanco drive west of the visitor center is a quick 5 miles to the wildlife-rich potholes of Red Tanks Tinaja and Pinkley Peaks picnic area. Toward the east is the Ajo Mountain loop drive, a beautiful 21-mile desert tour. It's a one-way road with no amenities, so stock up on fuel, water, food and sun protection before you begin. The loop offers amazing views

of barrel, saguaro and organ pipe cactuses. And in the spring, the desert floor can be filled with wildflowers such as orange poppies and purple lupine. If you keep a keen eye out, you also might see desert bighorn sheep, deer, coyotes and javelina.

The next morning, after happily photographing the sunrise, we head to Ranger Steve's house, where a blue enamel coffeepot is boiling on the stove. I have to admit I'm skeptical as I watch him add coffee grounds, two eggshells and a cinnamon stick.

After it has brewed, he hands me a mug, and I consider quietly dumping this crazy concoction into a nearby potted cactus. But after one sip I'm totally hooked. The flavor of it—like our experience in this extraordinary desert—is exotic, inviting and utterly unforgettable. ●

Spring rains coax Sonoran Desert poppies and lupines into glorious bloom.

STORY AND PHOTOS BY
DANA FOREMAN

VERDE VALLEY

EXPLORE ANCIENT RUINS, A QUIRKY MINING TOWN
AND TOWERING RED ROCKS.

WHEN PEOPLE LIVING in Phoenix need to get away from it all, they head 100 miles north to the Verde Valley and Sedona.

The lush Verde Valley is named for the Verde River, one of the last free-flowing rivers in the state. Several scenic roads lead visitors to the valley's wonders, which include sites preserving Native American history, old mining towns and red rock formations.

My friend Natalie Watson and I started our trip by walking beneath the cliff dwellings at Montezuma Castle National Monument. The site looks like an ancient apartment building and was home to the Sinagua people between A.D. 1100 and 1425. Although visitors can't climb up the ladders into the structure, we can imagine what living there must have been like. We then walked beside nearby Beaver Creek and relaxed in the peaceful, cool shade provided by a grove of sycamore trees.

By midday, we headed to the town of Jerome, which sits atop Cleopatra Hill. Jerome was once one of the richest copper mining camps in the world. Our visit to the Gold King Mine and Ghost Town was an adventure as we walked among old buildings, classic trucks and rusty mining tools.

As the sun dipped lower in the turquoise blue sky, we drove east for about 25 miles on state Route 89A, a curvy two-lane road, to visit Sedona's red rocks.

Natalie and I spent the next day hiking trails through Sedona. At Red Rock Crossing, I took photos of the iconic Cathedral Rock and waited for the last rays of the evening sun to hit the formation.

The next day was full of thrills. We climbed aboard at the Pink Jeep Plaza to go off-roading on the Broken Arrow Tour. Our Jeep climbed over rocks, making for a bumpy, magnificent experience for us.

On our last day, Natalie and I had one thing left to do: visit the Chapel of the Holy Cross, a church built into the red rocks. It was a lovely and serene end to our high-desert adventure. ◗

NOT TO BE MISSED

Head to the Sedona Airport Overlook to get a spectacular photo. It's where tourists gather to watch the sun set over the red rocks. The sight is unforgettable—a Kodak moment for sure.

Go bird-watching! The Verde Valley and Sedona are full of birding hot spots. Join Birding Northern Arizona for tours through riparian areas in Oak Creek Canyon, Sedona and Wet Beaver Creek, to name a few. Tours last from 3 hours to an entire day. Look for summer tanagers, yellow warblers, sparrows and many other birds.

Take a look at notes from the ancients. A short, easy stroll through the V Bar V Heritage Site leads to more than 1,000 petroglyphs. It's the largest collection of native rock art in the Verde Valley. *sedonaverde valley.org*

Top: Red Rock Crossing is the perfect spot to take in the beauty of Cathedral Rock. Bottom: Discover the Montezuma Castle National Monument.

A rainbow lights up the sky over the Rio Grande Gorge.

STORY BY
KARIN LEPERI

NORTHERN RIO GRANDE

GET TO KNOW AN ENIGMATIC LAND WITH TURQUOISE SKIES, TERRA-COTTA SOILS AND A TAPESTRY OF CULTURES.

THERE'S NO PLACE in the United States quite like northern New Mexico, especially the part of the state that is now designated as the Northern Rio Grande National Heritage Area. Much of the area's charm is due to the unique mix of vibrant native cultures with others who have settled here over hundreds of years.

Distinctively southwestern, the heritage area provides a one-of-a-kind glimpse into centuries of history, along with the stunning natural beauty of the area's high desert and mountain environment. Visiting the Northern Rio Grande is like traveling overseas without having to endure a cramped economy airline seat or breaking out your passport. And, in some cases, you may even feel transported back in time a few hundred years.

Stretching from Albuquerque to the Colorado border, the heritage area includes Santa Fe, Rio Arriba and Taos counties, encompassing a total of 10,000 square miles. Areas include those settled by the Jicarilla Apache,

the Tewa and Tiwa peoples, and by the descendants of Spanish colonists who arrived as early as 1598. To put it in perspective, that was a whole generation before the Pilgrims on the *Mayflower* landed at Plymouth Rock.

Today, the Northern Rio Grande is one of the newest additions to the National Park Service's heritage inventory, and it is truly a mosaic of the Americas. Take a few days to soak up the tapestry of its multicultural beginnings while enjoying the natural and varied scenery that includes deep gorges with exposed basalt, flat sandstone mesas, and rugged mountains with dramatic peaks and valleys. It's an unforgettable journey.

Start your exploration of the heritage area at the Santa Fe Plaza National Historic Landmark in downtown Santa Fe. The plaza, or city square, is symbolically the political and cultural center of Northern Rio Grande. Some say it is the heart of Santa Fe.

Known for its year-round open-air market, the plaza also hosts a variety

REST STOP

Tia Sophia's serves up some of the most in-demand New Mexican food on a value-priced menu. Popular with tourists and locals alike, this Santa Fe eatery is a delicious dining option. *tiasophias.com*

NOT TO BE MISSED

Taos Pueblo is a living community of people who choose to live the way their ancestors did for hundreds of years, surrounded by adobe walls without electricity or running water. This is the place to see ancient architecture combined with the culture of today's Pueblo people. *taospueblo.com*

See the Milky Way as you have never seen it before from the dark, unpolluted skies of northern New Mexico. One of the best places to stargaze is at Bandelier National Monument, where you can join night sky programs during the summer.

Learn about local artisans and their crafts at the Northern Rio Grande National Heritage Center. *riograndenha.org*

▼

On Good Friday, thousands come to El Santuario de Chimayo.

of special Native American and Spanish art markets, where traditional and contemporary works are for sale. Choose from a variety of jewelry, sculptures, pottery, textiles and handicrafts reflecting a mix of cultures. Also on the plaza is the Palace of the Governors, an adobe structure that is one of the oldest public buildings in the U.S. Prior to becoming a state museum in 1909, it was the seat of government under Spanish, Pueblo Indian, Mexican and U.S. territorial rule.

Then head north from Santa Fe along the storied High Road to Taos. This trek winds through gorgeous scenery (pinon and ponderosa pine woodlands offset by red rocks) in the Sangre de Cristo Mountains and past revered places that embody the mix of Spanish and Pueblo culture.

The first stop on this journey is Pojoaque, where you will find the Poeh Cultural Center and Museum. It's a repository with a special focus on the Tewa-speaking Pueblo communities: Pojoaque, San Ildefonso, San Juan, Santa Clara, Tesuque and Nambe.

The word *poeh* means "pathway" in the Tewa language, and the center lives up to its name as it connects the past with the present. The permanent collection tells the story of the Pueblo peoples and showcases many artistic treasures, including pottery returned by the Smithsonian Institution.

Farther along the road, churches founded in Spanish colonial times embrace all visitors. The faithful come to worship, while others bask in the serene beauty of the buildings and their natural setting. El Santuario de Chimayo, an adobe chapel that is a Good Friday destination for Holy Week pilgrims, is one such place. Built in 1813, the church also has tiny samples of healing earth, known to believers as *tierra bendita*.

Be sure to save plenty of time for Taos Pueblo, which is considered one of the oldest continuously inhabited places in the U.S. This Native American community was designated a UNESCO World Heritage Site in 1992. About 150 families live as their ancestors did in the multistory adobe structure. The local church, San Geronimo de Taos, is a lovely example of New Mexican architecture.

The red rocks and mountain terrain have inspired many who visit this area, including the painter Georgia O'Keeffe. Her home at Ghost Ranch in Abiquiu is tucked into the base of a mountain called Mesa Montosa. Dinosaur fossils embedded in colorful cliffs and sediment are found throughout the land. O'Keeffe painted extensively here, and her landscape paintings have gone on to become trademarks of sorts for northern New Mexico.

South of Abiquiu is Bandelier National Monument, an area of rugged canyons and mesas consisting of hundreds of Puebloan ruins and cave rooms carved into the soft, volcanic tuff rock. Of special note are the wooden ladders that give visitors an opportunity to climb up into the cavates (alcoves) themselves and imagine what it felt like to live in these cave rooms.

Bandelier is a favorite with hikers, as it covers about 50 square miles of ancient ruins, rock paintings and petroglyphs from the 12th through the 17th centuries. Wildlife watchers may spot birds and some of the park's 55 species of mammals, which include mule deer, Abert's squirrels and American badgers.

Additionally, photographers need to look no further than Bandelier for naturally illuminated scenery bathed in golden morning light. Dramatic cliffs at both the Frijoles Canyon and the

▼
Climb to the top of Tsankawi in Bandelier National Monument.

▼
The mighty Rio Grande flows through the national heritage area.

▼

Taos Pueblo is believed to be one of the oldest continuously inhabited settlements in the U.S.

Pajarito Plateau continually change their shape and color as filtered beams of sunshine play a contrasting game of lights and shadows. For a special curated experience, join a ranger-guided walk through the park or attend a talk during the summer and then stay for the evening campfire and night sky programs.

Another stop to add to your itinerary lies in the heart of the Sangre de Cristo Mountains, south of Santa Fe. Pecos National Historical Park has something to offer every interest. Here stand the remains of one of the most important pueblos in early New Mexico. It was the largest and most powerful due to its location, which made trade with the Plains Indians possible.

The Spanish arrived in 1540, which eventually led to the Franciscans establishing a mission and church in the early 1600s. Nowadays, the Spanish mission church is in ruins, but it is frequently photographed against dramatic skies and gives visitors a glimpse into the area's past.

The Pecos River flows through the park, and people cast fishing lines in spring and fall. Hikers trek trails (ranging from easy and paved to challenging) that wind past the ancestral sites of Pecos Pueblo and the glorious vistas of the mountains.

By exploring the Northern Rio Grande National Heritage Area, you experience a blend of American history, culture and landscape that is uniquely New Mexican. It's an area that celebrates the heritage of a diverse people who lived and settled in the area—from Apache and Pueblo peoples to Spanish colonists, Mexicans and even westward-bound pioneers. ●

STORY AND PHOTOS BY
TIM FITZHARRIS

PALO DURO CANYON

HIDDEN-IN-PLAIN-SIGHT WONDERS ARE WAITING TO BE DISCOVERED IN A TEXAN NATURAL TREASURE.

PALO DURO CANYON State Park is one of West Texas' most pleasant surprises. As you approach from Amarillo, it's mostly hidden from view—a sunken treasure with clear winding waters, red sandstone ramparts and graceful cottonwoods preserved in a glorious natural state.

The Prairie Dog Town Fork of the Red River carved out this canyon, which was likely discovered by early Spanish explorers. Palo Duro is Spanish for "hard wood"; the name may reflect the area's mesquite and juniper trees.

The federal Civilian Conservation Corps worked in the canyon from 1933 to 1937. Its young workers built road access to the canyon floor as well as a visitor center, cabins, shelters and the park headquarters.

The park, established in 1934, encompasses 29,182 acres of the northernmost section of the canyon. Palo Duro is often cited as the nation's second-largest canyon; it is roughly 120 miles long, up to 20 miles wide and more than 800 feet deep. Along the rim, the elevation measures 3,500 feet above sea level.

I reach for my camera as soon as the road begins its winding descent, opening up spectacular views. There are inspiring photo opportunities at nearly every turn, especially during the magical moments at dawn and dusk when the golden light plays over the soaring cliffs and rock spires.

I think one of the best features of Palo Duro is the interplay of blue sky, brick red rock and lime green riverside vegetation. To me, the scenery becomes even better in autumn, when the foliage turns fiery.

Palo Duro is also an ideal place to see wildlife, including the rare Texas horned lizard and Palo Duro mouse, as well as mule deer, wild turkeys and roadrunners.

The park has 30 miles of marked trails for hiking, biking or horseback riding. Visitors may ride their own horses, or Old West Stables provides guided trips to view the Lighthouse, the park's signature rock formation, on horseback. ◗

NOT TO BE MISSED

In June, July and August, the Pioneer Amphitheater on the canyon floor presents *Texas*, a musical about settlers of the Panhandle in the 1800s. *texas-show.com*

Horseback riders, mountain bikers, campers and picnickers can descend on the canyon for relaxation or adventure. The rim is the jumping-off point for a dramatic 8-mile drive to the canyon floor.

The park's signature rock formation, the Lighthouse, towers above the nearly 30,000 acres of dry washes, side canyons, honey mesquite and soapberry trees, and riverbeds shaded by cottonwoods.

FUN FACTS

The canyon is sometimes referred to as "The Grand Canyon of Texas." Artist Georgia O'Keeffe, who lived for a time in the Panhandle town of Canyon, described Palo Duro as "filled with dramatic light and color."

WORDS TO THE WISE

The park is open year-round and admission is charged. *palodurocanyon.com*

Top: Layers of red sandstone and gypsum color a bluff. Bottom: A Texas state longhorn grazes on the canyon rim.

The Lighthouse stands to the right of Castle Peak, both appropriately named rock formations.

"There are no vacant lots in nature."

—EDWARD ABBEY

MIDWEST
NORTHERN WISCONSIN WATERFALLS
PIPESTONE
Flint Hills
DOOR COUNTY
Silos & Smokestacks
ARROWHEAD
SLEEPING BEAR DUNES

▼

Sunflower fields brighten the landscape across Iowa's countryside.

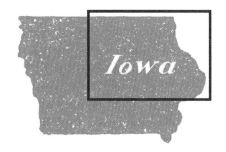

STORY BY
JEANNE AMBROSE

SILOS & SMOKESTACKS

VISIT TALLGRASS PRAIRIES WHERE BISON STILL ROAM AND
OLD-TIME FARMS WHERE THE SPIRIT OF THE PIONEERS LIVES ON.

THE PRAIRIE PUTS ON quite a show in the spring at the Neal Smith National Wildlife Refuge, about 22 miles east of Des Moines, Iowa. Butterflies flash their colors while flitting among the vivid wildflowers and the lofty grasses of the prairie. Bison calves frolic on their gangly legs near their mamas. Critters call out, and birds chatter and warble.

The refuge is one of more than 100 Iowa sites in the Silos & Smokestacks National Heritage Area being preserved and restored to show off the land's historical and cultural impact on early settlers. These living museums tell the story of how the native landscape influenced the evolution of agriculture in America. In Iowa, the sites tell tales of fields,

farmland, Native American farming practices, pioneer log homes with wood-burning cookstoves, and meadows and plains where herds of bison are being reestablished.

Volunteers and workers at the Neal Smith National Wildlife Refuge, established in 1990, are focused on restoring and protecting Iowa's prairies and oak savannas. Today, songbirds are making a robust comeback in Iowa due, in part, to places like the refuge.

"Birding is fabulous here," says Joan Van Gorp, president of the Friends of Neal Smith National Wildlife Refuge, a nonprofit group that supports the refuge. "Now the prairie attracts grassland birds we haven't seen for years, including bobolinks and the dickcissel."

REST STOPS

Fuel up at Goldie's Ice Cream Shoppe, a small old-timey diner not far from Neal Smith National Wildlife Refuge. Order the pork tenderloin. It's gargantuan and was voted the best in Iowa. Plus, Goldie's has pie! *goldiesice creamshoppe.com*

In northeast Iowa, about 20 miles south of Seed Savers Exchange, is the Little House on the Farm & Guest Barn bed and breakfast. There are two separate units right on the farm, so expect fresh eggs for breakfast and stunning stars in the clear night skies. *littlehouseonthe farm.com*

NEARBY ATTRACTIONS

Iowa has 1,600 miles of bike trails, making it the "world capital of trails." In Des Moines and the surrounding area alone, there are more than 550 miles of trails, including some craft brew bike routes. When you visit Seed Savers and the Laura Ingalls Wilder Museum, plan to ride the Trout Run Loop Trail, a scenic, paved 11-mile loop around Decorah.

▼

Visitors partake in a pioneer wedding at the Living History Museum.

More than 200 species of prairie plants have been seeded and nurtured at the refuge in an effort to preserve Iowa's prairie heritage. Bison and elk roam an 800-acre enclosure within the 5,600-acre refuge. I drove through the enclosure on the well-marked driving tour that visitors are encouraged to take—as long as they stay in their cars.

The refuge also includes miles of trails, the bison and elk enclosure, a butterfly garden, an oak savanna and the Prairie Learning and Visitor Center with knowledgeable volunteers, maps, a gift shop, historical exhibits, classrooms and a theater. Stop in at the Prairie Learning and Visitor Center so the volunteers can tip you off as to where the bison are hanging out. And bring your binoculars.

Living History Farms, a 500-acre hands-on museum in Urbandale, is another must-see site in the Silos & Smokestacks area. The immense outdoor "museum" captures the lifestyle of past generations. It includes log cabins, a print shop, a general store and a church, along with a working farm and a barn that houses hardworking Percheron draft horses. Best of all, visitors can experience a participatory stroll (or horse-drawn wagon ride) into the past, discovering how early settlers farmed, cooked and influenced the agriculture of Iowa's early farm country.

"People are used to museums that have collections under glass, but 85% of items in the Living History Farms collection are things we can carefully touch," says Janet Clair Dennis, director of interpretation. "It's a hands-on way to learn about history."

You can scrub clothes on an old-fashioned washboard, pick up an old iron or participate in one of the special events, like a traditional pioneer wedding. Or, catch an 1870s baseball game with rules that include no mitts, no cussin' and no spittin'. There's even an 1876 re-created town called Walnut Hill with active businesses where people dress in authentic period attire.

You can sign up for a historic skills class at Living History Farms, but plan ahead. Because of their authenticity, classes are limited in size. Check out *lhf.org* for upcoming events and dates at Living History Farms.

In the northeast corner of Iowa, just outside the city of Decorah, you'll find Seed Savers Exchange. This nearly 900-acre farm works to preserve America's food crops and gardens by collecting, growing, saving and storing heirloom seeds. It has a collection of more than 20,000 varieties of plants.

Start at the visitor center and explore Seed Savers' history. Wander the shop where you can buy seeds, garden tools and books, among other products. Hike the trails or fish in the trout stream. Best of all, linger

A short-eared owl hovers above the prairie.

▼
Open fields offer expansive views and ideal hiking terrain.

▼
Like a painting, the sky illuminates a red barn in Warren County, Iowa.

in the gorgeous display gardens and orchard with more than 900 varieties of apple trees.

Don't miss the library, which houses 6,000 volumes on agriculture, horticulture and biodiversity, some dating back to the 16th century. If you can't make the trip, go to *seedsavers.org* to shop for seeds or to learn how to save your own. You'll find a handy list of events, classes and hours of operation there, too.

About 8 miles north of Seed Savers Exchange is the Laura Ingalls Wilder Park & Museum. When the author was 9 years old, her family moved there to help a friend manage the Masters Hotel. This is her only childhood home that is still on its original site.

Stop in the visitor center across the street, the restored Burr Oak Savings Bank, to register for the guided tour

(lasting about an hour) of the hotel where Laura's family lived and worked from 1876 to 1877. While at the center, walk through the bank's original vault, hear stories of the county's first robbery, read Laura's letters to fans, and browse in the gift shop.

You may want to join the Laura Days Celebration in June (check dates online at *lauraingallswilder.us*) for children's pioneer games, food, a parade and crafts. Or dress up in pioneer costumes for a covered-wagon photo as a souvenir of your trip.

Wherever you decide to wander in Iowa—through prairie grasslands or sites that honor the past—you'll be walking in the footsteps of those pioneers who paved the way for the thriving agriculture and traditions thoughtfully preserved by the Silos & Smokestacks National Heritage Area. ●

Purple wildflowers carpet the prairie in Kansas' Flint Hills.

STORY BY
JENNIFER BROADSTREET HESS

FLINT HILLS

THIS AREA IN KANSAS BRIMS WITH BEAUTIFUL SMALL TOWNS, OLD WEST CHARM AND A TRAILBLAZING SENTIMENT.

MY IRISH ANCESTORS SETTLED in the Flint Hills of eastern Kansas in the late 1800s in hopes of finding a place to call their own. They were drawn to this land's lush rolling hills covered in verdant prairie grass, and the abundant wildflowers, native limestone rock formations and tranquil blue skies reminded them of home.

Five generations later, my family still lives in the Flint Hills. We're not alone among generations of pioneering families here who love the land and the people you can meet along state Route 177. Also known as the Kansas Flint Hills Scenic Byway, this drive winds north-south through the heart of the prairie. I have vivid childhood memories of traveling this road in our station wagon with the windows rolled down, inhaling fresh air and hearing meadowlarks sing. I think I have memorized every detail of the prairie's colors and patterns, relatively unchanged since the days when the American frontier was wide open.

Limestone buildings and fences line the old country roads. The underlying flinty limestone, which inspired the area's name, made it unattractive to crop farmers. Meanwhile, cattlemen established ranches and let their herds roam.

As a result, the Flint Hills is one of the largest unplowed tallgrass

REST STOP

Housed in the historic Rawlinson-Terwilliger Home in Council Grove, the Trail Days Cafe & Museum serves up dishes made with ingredients—such as bison—that Native Americans, settlers and farmers dined on. Take time to visit the museum as well. *traildayscafeand museum.org*

NOT TO BE MISSED

Located on the old Santa Fe Trail, the town of Council Grove has 25 historic sites to explore. The chamber of commerce offers a downloadable map to these sites, which are within walking distance. *councilgrove.com/ historicsites*

At the Tallgrass Prairie National Preserve, see one of the last remaining large stands of tallgrass prairie in the United States, learn about the Flint Hills ecosystem and tour historic ranch buildings. *nps.gov/tapr*

▼

Cattle roam one of the last remaining stands of tallgrass in the U.S.

prairie remnants in the world. And it's where the West began.

The scenic byway officially starts in the town of Council Grove. Under a stand of oak trees nearby, the Osage Nation signed a treaty with the U.S. government in 1825, ceding land along the Santa Fe Trail and promising a safe right of way. Ranging from Independence, Missouri, to Santa Fe, New Mexico, the trail brought pioneers to Council Grove on their way West.

This trail town on the Neosho River boasts 25 historical sites, and the Chamber of Commerce & Tourism offers a fun, educational map of all of them. My three kids, Jenevieve, James and Joeb, enjoyed charting the locations on the map as we walked most of the tour. The map also gives tidbits about the history of each place on the trail, like the Last Chance Store (so named because it was the last place to buy supplies for the trek between

Council Grove, Kansas and Santa Fe, New Mexico.

The Kaw Mission State Historic Site is another must-see. Built as a mission school to educate Native American children, about 30 orphaned Kaw boys stayed there from 1851 to 1854. Exhibits detail the history of the Flint Hills, the Kaw people (who were also known as the Kansa, hence the name Kansas), and the clashes between them and early European settlers.

About 20 miles south of Council Grove on Route 177 sits a sprawling historic ranch. I had driven by it many times with my grandparents, and our family always admired the ranch home and its outbuildings for their beautiful stonework and craftsmanship.

Built in 1878 by Stephen F. Jones, the Spring Hill Farm and Stock Ranch is now part of the Tallgrass Prairie National Preserve. Here, the past is honored and nature is protected. Visitors will see what life was like for folks living on this land in the 1880s. Explore the ranch's buildings, including its main house, limestone barn and the Lower Fox Creek School up on the hill. Other points of interest include an icehouse, outhouse, curing house and chicken pen.

The preserve holds one of the last stands of tallgrass prairie in the United States. Covering almost 11,000 acres of open space, it has miles of trails winding through the tallgrass. While hiking you may catch a glimpse from afar of the preserve's bison herd or their calves. To maintain a peaceful, tranquil atmosphere out on the prairie, no driving is allowed on the preserve, although a free tour bus is available.

Spring is our favorite time to visit the park, with its abundance of sunshine, blooming wildflowers and wildlife.

While the preserve is dedicated to the past, the town of Cottonwood Falls, about 5 miles south on Route 177, is a mix of old and new. The largest town in

▼
Rocks beneath the soil's surface made crop farming difficult here.

▼
Settlers passing through in the 1800s might have come upon a scene like this one at Tallgrass Prairie National Preserve.

▼

The Lower Fox Creek School held classes for one to 19 students until 1930.

Chase County, with a population of under 1,000, this ranching community was settled in 1854 when a trader named Seth Hays established a cattle ranch along the Cottonwood River near Diamond Spring Creek. Cattle drives, cowboys and the Old West are a legacy in Cottonwood Falls.

Broadway, the town's business hub, evokes a 19th-century feel with its brick streets and historic buildings, including the Chase County Courthouse. Built out of locally quarried limestone in 1872, the courthouse is really hard to miss, sitting atop a hill and displaying French Renaissance architecture. The courthouse is the oldest one still in use west of the mighty Mississippi River.

The first time my family visited, we were reluctant to explore because court was in session! But the employees are welcoming and love to share the building's history with visitors. A gorgeous three-story walnut staircase leads to the old jail on the second floor, and a window on the third floor offers a scenic view of the town below. My children gleefully discussed sliding down that amazing banister. Since I wanted to visit again, I nixed that idea quickly.

After touring the courthouse, discover all that Broadway has to offer: art galleries, antique stores, museums, restaurants and loads of weekend entertainment.

At the Flint Hills Gallery, find landscape paintings in which local artists capture the sunsets, stormy skies and ranching lifestyle of the region. Or listen to live music Friday evenings at Flint Hills Arts & Crafts, located inside the artists' cooperative Prairie PastTimes.

▼

Bison once grazed in this area in large numbers.

For an Old West experience, visit the Grand Central Hotel & Grill. This two-story brick hotel, centrally located in the downtown district, was originally opened in 1884 by M.M. Young. Always run as a hotel, it changed names over the years, closed for a decade and reopened in 1995. The interior is cowboy decor with traditional oak accents. Each of its 10 rooms features a historic brand from nearby ranches.

The Grand Central Hotel & Grill restaurant is widely known in the Flint Hills for its top-notch steaks, fried chicken and, in my opinion, the best onion rings (hand-dipped, crunchy and flavorful) in this part of the county.

If you're here in mid-June, come and experience Symphony in the Flint Hills. The Kansas City Symphony performs out on the prairie in this annual event.

Before the concert begins, you can stroll in the tallgrass, watch cowboys and cowgirls show their riding and herding skills, take a covered wagon ride, feast on barbecue or learn more about the area's ecosystem.

In the evening, relax and listen to music as the sun sets over the hills. But be forewarned: As the musicians play "Home on the Range," a herd of cattle is driven across the prairie. This tradition has been known to tug at the ol' heartstrings, awakening a sense of pride and patriotism in the audience.It's a truly spiritual experience, this combination of art, science, life and nature.

All along Route 177, you'll find friendly, tightknit communities where neighbors are more than willing to help each other, share their garden's bounty and live a simpler life. You might encounter horseshoe tournaments, street dances and watermelon feeds.

In the Flint Hills, the pioneer spirit lives on in the people, history and wide-open spaces. ❧

The original Teter Rock was erected as a guidepost for travelers on the prairie.

STORY AND PHOTOS BY
PAT AND CHUCK BLACKLEY

SLEEPING BEAR DUNES

TRAVERSE LAKE MICHIGAN'S SHORELINE FOR SUN,
SAND AND SPECTACULAR WATERFRONT VISTAS.

WITH ITS CRYSTAL BLUE WATER, miles of sandy beach, towering bluffs, immense sand dunes, wildflowers and 100 miles of hiking trails, Sleeping Bear Dunes National Lakeshore is one of the most enchanting areas we've ever visited. Located in northwestern Michigan on the shoreline of Lake Michigan, its 71,000 acres invite exploration.

When glaciers moved into this area from the north, they pushed rock and sand, gouging the earth. As the temperatures warmed and the glaciers began to retreat, they left behind landforms that filled with meltwater, creating the five Great Lakes and smaller inland lakes. Millennia later, wind, ice and water still reshape this marvelous landscape.

We arrived in late May, hoping to photograph spring wildflowers, and we weren't disappointed when we set off with maps we picked up at the Philip A. Hart Visitor Center in Empire, along with advice from rangers.

Our first hike took us to Pyramid Point, a bluff with great views of Lake Michigan and the Manitou Islands. The trek took us through a beech-maple forest with blooms like bellwort and Dutchman's breeches. We even found a very rare green and white trillium.

On the popular Empire Bluff Trail, we found more wildflowers, including jack-in-the-pulpits, violets and trout lilies, as well as trillium and squirrel corn. Perched 450 feet above the lakeshore, the overlook provides breathtaking views.

The 7.4-mile Pierce Stocking Scenic Drive is another way to take in the park, with 12 stops that offer lake and dune vistas. At the Lake Michigan Overlook, a short walk brought us to the perfect spot for sunset photos as the sun dropped over the sparkling waters.

Our favorite experience was the Dune Climb, a vigorous hike up a 110-foot-high sand dune perched on a bluff. We arrived before dawn and watched the sunrise turn the clouds pink and light up the dune grasses.

A sandhill crane appeared, winding through the sand. He left behind footsteps and two happy photographers captivated by Sleeping Bear Dunes. ◗

FUN FACTS

The name Sleeping Bear Dunes comes from a Native American story about the largest dune in the park, called Mother Bear. At that time, the dune looked like a bear at rest.

The area includes hiking and biking trails, two offshore islands, a maritime museum and a lighthouse. *sleepingbeardunes.com*

WORDS TO THE WISE

Bring a pair of shoes if you plan to hike on the dunes. While the sand might feel nice on your bare feet at first, the National Park Service warns that the sand can be hot and abrasive.

NEARBY ATTRACTIONS

Cruise down the 7.4-mile Pierce Stocking Scenic Drive to soak up the scenery, especially at the Lake Michigan Overlook. At nearly 450 feet above the lake, the overlook offers breathtaking views of the Sleeping Bear Dunes far away in the distance. And, for those who aren't keen on a long walk, the overlook is just a short hike from the parking lot.

Top: Hikers relax along the Empire Bluff Trail. Bottom: This iconic barn at D.H. Day farm is a local landmark.

Split Rock Lighthouse stands as a sentinel on a 130-foot cliff above the rocky shore of Lake Superior.

STORY BY
KELSEY ROSETH

ARROWHEAD

EACH SUMMER, MINNESOTANS HEAD TO THIS REGION, A LAND OF LUSH FORESTS, TRANQUIL WATERS AND NATURAL WONDERS.

PEACEFUL, SCENIC HIKING TRAILS. Towering Norway pines mixed with white-barked paper birch trees. Miles of water highways connecting tranquil lakes and winding rivers to sun-dappled Lake Superior. These are the natural characteristics that drew me to Minnesota's Arrowhead region.

So named because of its shape, the Arrowhead region in northeast Minnesota became my home six years ago when I moved here from Fargo, North Dakota. I went from being surrounded by rich, fertile farmlands to being nestled amid thick forests and craggy rock formations. Here, Superior National Forest, which spans more than 3 million acres, links the vast Boundary Waters Canoe Area Wilderness to the stunning North Shore of Lake Superior.

The Arrowhead was an ideal choice for an adventure-seeker like me. Among the tall pines of boreal forests and the calm waters of the state's lakes and rivers, I experience gratitude daily. This is God's country.

With each twist and turn of the North Shore Scenic Drive, a 142-mile byway from Duluth to the Canadian border, explorers see natural wonders and learn about the area's rich mining, lumber and fur-trading history.

The drive, established in the early 1900s, follows the rugged shoreline of Lake Superior and serves as the starting point for thousands of adventures. Each year, more than 3 million visitors make their way here, including my North Dakota relatives. I often take out-of-town guests along the North Shore so they, too, can experience the sheer magnificence of this place.

One of the first towns along the Scenic Drive is Two Harbors, a popular destination for watching 1,000-foot iron ore freight ships navigate the port at Agate Bay. Both "lakers" (ships from the Great Lakes) and "salties" (vessels from across the world) load up here before heading on to steel mills.

About 15 miles past Two Harbors is Gooseberry Falls State Park, one of

NOT TO BE MISSED

The 142-mile North Shore Scenic Drive has gorgeous views of Lake Superior and abounds with small-town charm. Look for moose along the 57-mile Gunflint Trail National Scenic Byway. Explore the waterfalls along the river in Gooseberry Falls State Park. Put your oar in and paddle through tranquil waters at the Boundary Waters Canoe Area Wilderness. And take a guided boat tour of Voyageurs National Park, named in honor of French-Canadian fur traders.

FUN FACT

The common loon is Minnesota's state bird. Though somewhat clumsy on land, these birds are excellent swimmers. Their call is the song of summer in the Arrowhead.

▼

About 12,000 loons make their summer home in Minnesota.

Minnesota's most popular parks, with about 900,000 visitors annually. The densely forested park contains evergreens, aspens and birches alongside an impressive river gorge, which has jutting rocks carved by basalt lava flows more than 1 billion years ago. I like to visit often, exploring scenic overlooks, historic log buildings and the park's three majestic waterfalls: the Upper, Middle and Lower Falls of the Gooseberry River.

A short drive later, travelers see a sight that was welcomed by many sailors of long ago: Split Rock Lighthouse. This icon of the North Shore is perched on a sharp, 130-foot cliff and surrounded by a state park. Built in 1909, it was operated by on-site lightkeepers for about 60 years. Today, the Minnesota Historical Society owns the lighthouse, employing an on-site manager. Take a tour, learn its history and get an up-close look at the 1,000-watt bulb.

Farther along the North Shore you'll find more gems, including Tettegouche State Park, which is known for vistas, miles of hiking and cross-country skiing trails, and a shoreline littered with colorful agate rocks. At about the 109-mile mark, you'll reach Grand Marais, a charming art-centric harbor community. Feel the cool breeze off the lake as you dine in restaurants with locally sourced food, or shop in one of the art galleries or small stores dotting the downtown. Grand Marais serves as the gateway to the remote Gunflint Trail, a 57-mile national scenic byway that leads adventurers to the Boundary Waters Canoe Area Wilderness. There are no towns along this winding two-lane road, which has some of the best moose-spotting opportunities in the whole state.

On the northern half of the state's Arrowhead region is Boundary Waters Canoe Area Wilderness, located southeast of Voyageurs National Park.

The Gunflint Trail is known for pristine lakes, including West Bearskin Lake, seen here from the Caribou Rock Trail.

▼
Gooseberry Falls State Park is a popular destination thanks to its breathtaking vistas and waterfalls.

Canoeists paddle along the Kelso River in Boundary Waters Canoe Area Wilderness.

This area, known for being a natural mosaic of land and water, covers more than 1 million acres intersected by about 1,200 miles of canoe routes.

Routes range in difficulty from the one-day, entry-level Isabella Lake route, where paddlers easily meander past rugged islands, sandy beaches and rocky shoals, to more challenging routes such as the Frost River Loop. Typically, only experienced canoeists attempt this remote loop, taking part in a challenging excursion in which paddlers often catch a glimpse of loons, river otters, coyotes, foxes, moose and bobcats.

My husband, George, and I find immense comfort in exploring the quiet of this place. With the exception of a few lakes, motors are not allowed, which means that canoes and kayaks are the main mode of transportation.

While on leisurely laps around these lakes, George and I take time to appreciate how birds chirp and sing in the distance, and how frog croaks reach a crescendo as we near the banks of the water. The dichotomy of the Boundary Waters is significant. There is peace and stillness here, yet the rugged landscape and immense isolation require its visitors to have strength, endurance and definitely some outdoor survival skills.

Though we've lived here for years, my husband and I are still called to further explore the Arrowhead. We crave the chance to spot a 6-foot-tall moose, watch a bald eagle taking flight, or otherwise marvel at the juxtaposed tranquility and energy of this region. This is indeed God's country, and we hope to never leave it. ❧

▼

Winnewissa Falls tumbles 20 feet into a pretty wooded canyon.

STORY AND PHOTOS BY
LAURENCE PARENT

PIPESTONE

FIND OUT WHY THIS UNIQUE PRAIRIE OASIS HAS BEEN
SACRED TO NATIVE AMERICANS FOR 3,000 YEARS.

AFTER A QUICK TOUR of the Pipestone National Monument visitor center in southwest Minnesota, our kids run out the door, eager to see the Native American rock quarries for which the park is named. The three-quarter-mile Circle Trail leads us toward a reddish rock bluff under skies darkening with the threat of thunderstorms.

According to the National Park Service, this is perhaps the highest-quality, best-known deposit of pipestone in the world. For thousands of years, the Sioux, Pawnee, Crow, Blackfoot and other tribes have carved ceremonial pipes and other crafts from this durable, easily shaped red metamorphic clay stone. Many revered this place as sacred ground, believing that the smoke from their pipes carried their prayers to the Great Spirit.

The trail passes several small, overgrown quarry pits as it wanders between tallgrass prairie and patches of woods. Before long we reach a small wooded canyon carved out by the rushing waters of Pipestone Creek. The path follows the creek between low quartzite cliffs amid the growing roar of water tumbling down Winnewissa Falls. It's a pretty little waterfall, and quite a surprise here in the middle of the prairie.

Then the trail climbs back up onto the grassland and leads us past active stone quarries where Native Americans still use picks, shovels, sledgehammers and wedges to extract the thin layers of pipestone from thick, hard layers of Sioux quartzite rock. Only Native Americans who are enrolled in a tribe recognized by the U.S. government are allowed to quarry pipestone, and then only by permit. Currently there is a five- to six-year waiting period to obtain a permit.

No power tools are allowed, so it's a slow, laborious process that can take two to six weeks. First, up to 6 feet of

NOT TO BE MISSED

Visit the exhibit quarry, where you can see an actual quarry from the bottom in which the floor and lower wall are pipestone.

In the cultural center, local carvers demonstrate how they work with pipestone. Many of their finished items are for sale in the visitor center gift shop.

FUN FACT

The 300-acre Pipestone National Monument was established by Congress in 1937. The legislation contains a provision that guarantees the right of Native Americans to continue quarrying pipestone. This legislation is in effect today.

WORDS TO THE WISE

The site is open daily, except on major holidays. *nps.gov/pipe*

NEARBY ATTRACTION

Visit the 1890s in downtown Pipestone. It boasts a wealth of lovingly preserved Sioux quartzite buildings. *pipestone minnesota.com*

▼

Centuries of labor went into this tailings pile.

soil has to be dug up and carted away in wheelbarrows. Then chisels and wedges are used to break loose blocks of rock from quartzite layers that range from 4 to 10 feet thick. After those blocks are pried loose and dropped to the quarry floor, the quarrymen break them up with sledgehammers into chunks small enough to cart away.

The 10- to 18-inch-thick seam of pipestone is composed of fragile layers 1.5 to 3 inches thick. The quarrymen drive wedges into the soft rock's natural horizontal seams, then they carefully remove the pipestone in flat, irregularly shaped slabs.

A few drops of rain begin to spatter us, quickly followed by a downpour, so we run back to the visitor center to watch a Native American artisan carve the stone into pipes. He explains that the tools have improved through the centuries, but the meaning of this sacred ritual remains the same.

Thanks to this surprising, beautiful little park, we get the chance to feel a bit of that spiritual connection to the land, the sky and the gifts they share. ●

A thunderstorm looms on the prairie.

Winter brings peace and quiet to Ellison Bluff County Park.

STORY BY
CHERYL RODEWIG

DOOR COUNTY

THE OFF-SEASON IN THIS NORTHEAST WISCONSIN PENINSULA HOLDS UNEXPECTED CHARMS FOR NATURE LOVERS.

I ALMOST MISS IT. A pre-dawn excursion is all the harder when the weather is cold and the previous night's revelry (in my case, a Scandinavian banquet with drinking songs) kept me up later than usual.

But I prevail. Slipping away from the comfort of my bayside inn, I reach the eastern-facing Cave Point County Park just in time to see the early morning darkness recede before a blushing sky. Waves from Lake Michigan batter the shore, where icicles cling to dolomite cliffs carved with sea caves—hidden depths for kayakers and divers to explore.

Some of the water escapes through blowholes, erupting into the air like geysers. I get too close trying to take a photo and get doused, but I don't care. I have the place to myself, and it's glorious—the perfect culmination of my trip to Wisconsin's Door County.

I'd spent the previous two days on the peninsula tramping through some of the state's most idyllic winter landscapes. Better known as a bustling summertime retreat, Door County's double-sided shoreline draws sunbathers and surfers June through August, when the weather peaks in the pleasant mid-70s. It's sometimes called the Cape Cod of the Midwest, with the beaches, lighthouses and seafood shacks to prove it. But I like it in the winter—uncrowded, quiet and pristine, especially after the fresh snowfall that arrived on my first night, right on cue.

My introduction to Door County's very scenic off-season begins at Whitefish Dunes State Park. The beachfront park turns snowy November through March, when you can trade in your swimsuit for snowshoes. Though when I visit in early December, I'm told it's not yet deep enough for snowshoes. I'm disappointed at first, but only briefly. Once inside the park, I'm surrounded by the postcard panoramas that I was hoping for: towering hardwoods like oak, beech and maples intermixed with evergreens, all comfortably blanketed in white.

REST STOP

Al Johnson's Swedish Restaurant & Butik is famous for two things: live goats on the sod roof and Scandinavian cuisine. In winter, the goats are replaced with lighted reindeer, but the food is never better than during the *julbord* in December. The menu serves up herring, lox, potato sausage, cheeses, *julskinka* (Swedish Christmas ham) and much more. *aljohnsons.com*

NOT TO BE MISSED

Celebrate the holidays with Christmas in the Village, an annual daylong celebration in Ephraim for caroling, carriage rides, a tree lighting and the chance to meet Saint Nick. Visitors can also discover Ephraim's rich Norwegian heritage through old-fashioned games and Moravian holiday displays. *ephraim-doorcounty.com*

In a 19th-century church, the Tannenbaum Holiday Shop, a year-round store, sells every kind of Christmas decor. *tannenbaum holidayshop.com*

▼

Sherwood Point Lighthouse guided sailors into Sturgeon Bay.

I begin on the Yellow Trail, branching off from the Green Trail to head down to the creek. It is slow going for me, not because of the terrain, which is fairly flat, but because I stop every few minutes to snap a photo. The Yellow is one of three cross-country skiing trails and is the longest at more than 4 miles. Ice fishing, another favorite winter pastime, is possible at Clark Lake. The park even has a program to loan out fishing poles and tackle free of charge (be sure to check with the park beforehand).

I stick to hiking, finishing the loop before heading north to an outdoor escape of a different kind. Bjorklunden (meaning "Birch Grove" in Swedish) is the northern campus of Lawrence University. The tranquil setting seems well-suited to contemplation. And if the landscape isn't as dramatic as Whitefish Dunes, Bjorklunden has something the state park doesn't: a replica of a Norwegian *stavkirke* from the 12th century.

This is what I came for. I follow a short trail from the campus lodge, arriving at a small clearing to find Boynton Chapel, looking every bit the fairy tale with its dark exterior and woodland backdrop. Blue-toned stained glass glimmers in the windows.

The scalloped eaves end in dragon heads, which are thought to ward off evil. It's one of two stavkirkes in the county. The second, located on Washington Island which is about 30 miles north, is another reproduction that was built to honor Door County's early Scandinavian immigrants.

If I want to venture farther, I'll need skis or snowshoes. While the other trails are open, they are ungroomed in winter. But evening comes early, and I want to make the most of daylight. I still have one final stop on the other side of Baileys Harbor.

At 1,600 acres, The Ridges Sanctuary outdoes my other stops of the day in sheer scale—it's nearly twice the size of Whitefish Dunes and four times that of Bjorklunden.

Wisconsin's first land trust has miles of trails winding among hearty conifers that form a boreal forest rare for this latitude. White spruce and balsam fir flourish, as do even irises and orchids in warmer months. A naturalist tells me the birdsong is hard to ignore in the spring.

But now, all is still, the silence echoing in the stark architecture of the trees and frozen swales. I hike to the end of my chosen trail, where two 19th-century range lights stand sentinel at opposite ends of a long path.

The lighthouses, which once helped sailors avoid the harbor's dangerous shallows, are rather picturesque today; the boardwalk to reach them is uncluttered by footprints in the snow.

I wish I could stay longer, but it's time to wind down (in true Wisconsin style, with a fish boil at a Victorian bed-and-breakfast). I'll need to rest up for tomorrow when I tackle the western shore, which includes Door County's largest preserve, Peninsula State Park, prized for its snowmobile trails overlooking Green Bay.

I take one last look at the range lights, snapping one more photo to capture the memory—winter beauty, after all, is evanescent—and I retrace my footsteps toward the trailhead. ●

▼
A hiker carefully treks through snow at Cave Point County Park.

STORY AND PHOTOS BY
THEODORE SADLER

NORTHERN WISCONSIN WATERFALLS

REFLECT AND RECHARGE WHILE EXPLORING CASCADING WATERS IN THE MAJESTIC FORESTS OF THE NORTH WOODS.

SEEKING OUT THE WATERFALLS of Iron County, Wisconsin, is the perfect weekend getaway. Located on the northern edge of the state, Iron County borders Michigan's Upper Peninsula and the mighty Lake Superior.

I left my home in Minneapolis early Saturday morning and drove about four hours to my first trip destination, scenic Copper Falls State Park.

Along the way I drove past the huge pines of the Chequamegon-Nicolet National Forest. The trees, the deep blue sky, the incandescent sun and the cool air of Wisconsin's North Woods invigorated my spirit.

That day I explored the marvels of Copper Falls and its neighbor, Brownstone Falls. The 1.7-mile Doughboys Trail winds around both waterfalls, offering lovely views.

The park is home to many falls and to rustic log buildings and trails constructed in the 1930s by the Civilian Conservation Corps. You can hike,

mountain bike, fish or swim in the park (Loon Lake has 300 feet of beach).

With ease and a relaxed pace, I continued my journey northeast about 15 miles on state Highway 169 to Potato River Falls, where I stood in awe before what some consider to be the state's most beautiful cascade. Next up was Saxon Falls, then Superior Falls, both just over the Michigan border.

The day ended with a short drive into Ashland, Wisconsin, where I stayed at a hotel overlooking the marina. A thunderstorm struck in the pre-dawn hours, affording me spectacular photos.

After an early breakfast, I headed out to my last stop: Morgan Falls. While very remote and a tad out of the way, this final waterfall was well worth the effort. At the end of a short hike on a wide, flat path, Morgan Falls looks like something created for an amusement park. As I bid farewell to my waterfall weekend, I already begin planning my return trip. ❧

REST STOP

Known as "the mural capital of Wisconsin," Ashland is a good place to eat, stay and play while visiting the area's waterfalls. Tour the eight-block historic Main Street and experience the town's history and culture through the murals painted on the buildings.

NOT TO BE MISSED

Copper Falls State Park is a real gem located near Lake Superior in northern Wisconsin. Waterfalls, gorges, and hiking and mountain biking trails await visitors. Hike 4 miles of the North Country National Scenic Trail, which stretches from North Dakota to Vermont. *dnr.wi.gov*

NEARBY ATTRACTION

See the Ashland Breakwater Lighthouse, one of the few lighthouses built using reinforced concrete. It stands at the end of a long breakwater in Lake Superior. Although there are no tours, the lighthouse is accessible by boat.

Top: Tyler Forks River forms scenic cascades in Copper Falls State Park. Bottom: The Ashland Breakwater Lighthouse is still operational.

The sky paints a peaceful scene over the Ashland Marina in Wisconsin at sunset.

" *In every outthrust headland, in every curving beach, in every grain of sand there is a story of the earth.*"

—RACHEL CARSON

SOUTHEAST

WAKULLA SPRINGS

APPALACHIAN FOREST

COASTAL SCENIC

CONNECTION BYWAY

RED RIVER GORGE

ATCHAFALAYA BASIN

BURKE'S GARDEN

GULLAH GEECHEE

LINVILLE GORGE WILDERNESS

NEWTON COUNTY

CATALOOCHEE VALLEY

▼

The shores are calling from Dauphin Island to Orange Beach, where the sun, sand and surf await.

STORY BY
SARA BROERS

COASTAL CONNECTION SCENIC BYWAY

OCEAN VIEWS, WILDLIFE AND HISTORY BECKON VISITORS
TO THIS SUNNY SOUTHERN COAST.

TAKE A DRIVE ALONG PART of Alabama's Coastal Connection Scenic Byway and experience pristine beaches, historical sites, abundant nature and fabulous meals. Begin your tour on Dauphin Island, head east on state Route 180 to Gulf Shores and wrap it up in Orange Beach after exploring the many intriguing sites along this coastal gem. Plan on spending a minimum of two days, because the beauty of this area will certainly lure you in.

Fort Gaines is on Dauphin Island and has guarded the entrance to Mobile Bay for 150 years. After exploring this historic site, there's nothing like driving onto the Mobile Bay Ferry for an epic float over to Gulf Shores. Dolphins, jellyfish and pelicans will keep your eyes glued to your binoculars as you cross the bay. Make your first stop Fort Morgan, located on Mobile Point. Both Fort Gaines and Fort Morgan have small entrance fees and offer interactive experiences as well as panoramic views of the bay area. Fort Morgan is also a prime birding location. Plan to spend a

POINTS *of* INTEREST

REST STOPS

Lucy Buffett's Lulu's Gulf Shores offers fresh seafood, bread pudding and a family fun zone area. And if food allergies are an issue, Lulu's has you covered. *lulubuffett. com/gulf-shores*

For a burger on the beach, head to The Gulf in Orange Beach for locally sourced beef paired with house-cut fries. And the shrimp tacos can't be beat! *thegulf.com*

To sleep tight, Jus Jammin through Lucky Bird Vacations offers a clean, comfortable place to call home in Gulf Shores. Turquoise Place in Orange Beach is a beachfront property with a personal hot tub in each unit overlooking the Gulf of Mexico. The Beach Club near Fort Morgan offers a beachfront property in a secluded area. The Tides Hotel in Orange Beach, a Best Western Premier hotel, has terrific views of the tides. Young's Suncoast Realty & Vacation Rentals offers one- and three-bedroom condos at The Wharf, a popular gathering spot. *gulfshores.com/ lodging*

▼

Go bird-watching at Bon Secour National Wildlife Refuge.

minimum of two hours at each of these historic sites.

Travel on to the Bon Secour National Wildlife Refuge in Gulf Shores. This area is home to countless migratory birds and the endangered Alabama beach mouse. Look for loggerhead, green and Kemp's ridley sea turtles. With more than 360 different species of birds, this is a bird lover's paradise. The Jeff Friend Loop Trail is a nice level hike through a coastal marsh and forestland. The trail is wheelchair friendly, with benches along the way for relaxing and taking in the view. If you are a nature fan, you can easily spend a full day in the Bon Secour National Wildlife Refuge. Be sure to bring your binoculars, bug spray, sunscreen and fresh water.

Kayak fishing with Whistlin' Waters Outdoors is one of the best ways to explore the marshlands along the coast. Scott or Bill will guide you through this beautiful area and help you snag the "catch of a lifetime." Along with getting a little exercise as you paddle your kayak through the bay, this is another incredible bird-watching opportunity. Book your kayak fishing experience for early in the day, when the waters are quiet and you can hear the wildlife.

The ultimate view of Alabama's Gulf Shores can be found from above, so book a flight with Beach Flight Aviation. Gary will help you feel comfortable as you board the gyroplane. I opted to fly over Fort Morgan. The turquoise waters along the beaches of Alabama are a sight that I will remember forever. The view of the byway from the sky is out of this world and worth every moment in flight.

The pristine beaches of Gulf Shores will soothe your soul as well as your feet. There is public beach access in Gulf Shores with ample parking. During the hot summer season, though, the parking lot fills quickly, so plan to arrive early. There are also restroom and shower facilities. A range of beachfront lodging is nearby as well, from condos to camping.

While in Orange Beach, explore the oceanfront from the Cotton Bayou Public Beach Access, where you'll find showers, free parking and fishing charters. Be sure to check with local guidelines and websites for current information, closings and changing traveling conditions.

If you have to choose only one coastal road trip to make in the coming year, choose Alabama's Coastal Connection. You will not regret the slower pace and the inviting scenery waiting for you in this southern paradise.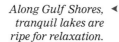

Along Gulf Shores, ◄ tranquil lakes are ripe for relaxation.

▼

A lookout tower offers this stunning view of Arkansas' Grand Canyon.

STORY BY
KIMBERLY LISS

NEWTON COUNTY

WHEN FALL'S SPLENDOR ARRIVES IN THE OZARK MOUNTAINS OF ARKANSAS, IT'S TIME TO HIT THE TRAILS.

FOR THREE GLORIOUS FALL DAYS, my family takes a trip south to Newton County, Arkansas, to hike the many trails and view some of the prettiest scenery in the Southeast.

Vibrant hues of red, yellow, gold, orange and even purple cover the trees. Autumn puts on an amazing show here.

The nights are cool and crisp, but the days are still warm enough to wear just a light long-sleeved shirt or T-shirt and jeans. While hiking, we've even seen a few snakes warming themselves in the hot afternoon sun.

We usually stay in Jasper, a small town of about 430 residents, which is surrounded by stunning natural beauty. The Buffalo National River, the first national river in the U.S., flows nearby. There are plenty of recreational opportunities in this stretch of the Ozark Mountains, including hiking, canoeing, kayaking, fishing and hunting.

Our passion is hiking, and we do a lot of it. The trail at Lost Valley, near Boxley Valley and 2 miles southwest of Ponca on state Highway 43, is an especially gorgeous and easy hike. The trail is a little over 2 miles long with plenty of scenery to behold and cliffs and large boulders to climb. We sometimes hike up the creek bed, which is mostly dry, and clamber over the large rocks and cascading ledges. Cob Cave has a giant overhang just above the creek. Evidence of corncobs left by Native Americans have been found there, hence its name.

At the far end of the Lost Valley is Eden Cave, which leads to Eden Falls. If you bring a flashlight and can manage the 30-foot crawl to the back of the cave, you are rewarded with a trickling 30-foot waterfall. Bats can be seen in the cave, so please be courteous and do not bother them. Also, don't forget to duck—the ceilings can be low!

REST STOPS

Rent one of Cliff House Inn's five rooms and wake up each morning to an amazing view of Arkansas' Grand Canyon. On a clear day you can see for miles. It's simply breathtaking. Upstairs at the restaurant, be sure to try the Company's Comin' Pie, with a meringue crust, whipped cream and crushed pineapple. *cliffhouseinnar.com*

The Ozark Cafe is on the square across from the old county courthouse in Jasper. The cafe is more than 100 years old, and you'll understand why it is still in business—plenty of hearty food, great service and live music on Saturdays. *ozarkcafe.com*

The Arkansas House, a two-story historic building, has been around a long time. It's a beautiful landmark with gorgeous rooms for an overnight stay. *thearkhouse.com*

Need a sweet treat? The goodies at Blue Mountain Bakery never disappoint, especially after a long hike. *bluemountain bakery.com*

Get to know the deepest canyon in the Ozarks.

Boxley Valley is rich in history and has been made even more famous by its local inhabitants: elk. The animals were once numerous in this region; however, by the 1840s, they were all gone. Elk from the Rocky Mountains were introduced into the area in 1981. Visitors come here year-round to watch the herds. There are spots where you can pull over and photograph the elk in the valley.

Farther south in Boxley Valley, down several miles of a road that alternates from red clay to dirt and gravel, is the trail leading to Hawksbill Crag, a rock formation that extends out from the cliff and resembles a hawk's beak. The trek is rugged, but the view of miles of Ozark beauty is so worth the effort.

For history buffs, there are lovely old homesites, churches and cemeteries to explore in Boxley Valley, as well as many hiking trails along the Buffalo River. Bordered by towering cliffs, the river's clear, cold water draws crowds of canoers and campers year-round.

The hamlet of Ponca, located on the northern edge of Boxley Valley, boasts a lodge, cabins, the Elk Education Center, a convenience store and several residences.

Make a visit to Newton County, and you won't be disappointed. Be sure to bring comfortable hiking shoes and your camera!

▼
The multi-tiered Eden Falls is a must-see.

▼
Cypress wetlands around Wakulla Springs are home to abundant wildlife.

STORY BY
PIPER SCHAD

WAKULLA SPRINGS

DIVE INTO THE SUNSHINE STATE'S BEST SWIMMING HOLE.

IF YOU'RE ON A JOURNEY through the Florida Panhandle, consider stopping in Wakulla Springs.

Located south of Tallahassee, Wakulla Springs is the state's largest and deepest freshwater spring and is protected within Edward Ball Wakulla Springs State Park.

Each day, more than 200 million gallons of water flow through the 185-foot-deep spring. At the designated swimming area, where the water stays frigid at about 70 degrees year-round, lifeguards oversee kids jumping off the 20-foot diving platform—and make sure no one sneaks into the roped-off area, where they may encounter an alligator.

The unique swimming hole is quite impressive, but it's just one of many reasons to visit. There's also the area's film history, plentiful wildlife and super cool lodge.

In the 1940s and '50s, *Creature from the Black Lagoon* and the first Tarzan movie starring Johnny Weissmuller were filmed here. It's a testament to Wakulla Springs' truly wild and otherworldly landscape. Divers found an intact mastodon skeleton on the basin's floor in 1931, and scuba divers report seeing other fossils beneath the water's surface. That mastodon, an animal similar to an elephant, is on display nearby at the Museum of Florida History in Tallahassee.

After swimming in the incredibly clear, brisk water, you'll want to take the Jungle Cruise River Boat Tour. It's the best way to see the park's swamplands and amazing wildlife including alligators, turtles, birds, fish and, if you're lucky, manatees. On our boat tour, we saw about 20 alligators and a mother manatee

POINTS of INTEREST

NOT TO BE MISSED

Book a kayak or canoe tour with TNT Hideaway to observe manatees up close in the Wakulla River or to take a moonlight paddle. *tnthideaway.com*

St. Marks National Wildlife Refuge covers more than 80,000 acres of coastal marshes, islands, tidal creeks and estuaries. See alligators sunning in the wetlands and eagles flying overhead as you hike the trails. Migratory birds stop over in winter, making the refuge a global hot spot for birding. Hike to the beach and see St. Marks Lighthouse, fashioned of lime-stone blocks taken from the ruins of a 17th-century fort. The light has cast its beam into the night skies above the Gulf of Mexico since the early 1830s. *fws.gov/refuge/St_Marks*

The Tallahassee-St. Marks Historic Railroad State Trail is 16 miles of mostly paved path. Cyclists can follow it from the state capital to the beach in St. Marks.

▼

An anhinga, or snake bird, suns itself.

with her calf sliding through the shallow waters.

The Lodge at Wakulla Springs is an art deco treasure. Built in the 1930s by businessman Edward Ball, the lodge hearkens back to another era in Florida's history. The gift shop has a vintage soda fountain known for serving root beer floats and sundaes for shockingly cheap prices. The counter measures 70 feet, making it the longest marble soda fountain ever built.

You can easily explore Wakulla Springs in half a day, but half the fun is staying at this little hotel. The extensive marble, cypress wood and iron details give the 27-room lodge a feeling of old-school glamour. I can only imagine how cozy the fireplace can be.

Wakulla Springs is an excellent spot for nature lovers, film buffs or anyone searching for something unique and wild along America's back roads. ◖

▼

The historic Lodge at Wakulla Springs has 27 rooms and a vintage soda fountain.

STORY AND PHOTO BY
PAT & CHUCK BLACKLEY

RED RIVER GORGE

TRAVEL TO KENTUCKY'S ROCKY WONDERLAND OF STONE ARCHES, TOWERING CLIFFS AND PLUNGING RAVINES.

WITH MORE THAN 100 natural sandstone arches, Kentucky's Red River Gorge Geological Area boasts one of America's largest collections of these picturesque wonders.

Carved out of the Cumberland Plateau, the gorge, with its massive forested cliffs and narrow ravines, is part of the Daniel Boone National Forest and one of the state's most popular hiking areas. The Red River makes a fabulous avenue for canoeists and kayakers to wind their way through the gorge.

You can see many of the arches along the gorge's 60 miles of hiking trails. One of the most impressive and widely known, Sky Bridge, is easily reached via a scenic loop trail of less than a mile that offers awesome views into the gorge. The trail passes over and beneath this 75-foot-long, 23-foot-high natural stone bridge.

Sky Bridge and the other arches were sculpted by weather and water when their softer shale and siltstone layers eroded away, leaving only the harder sandstone layers standing the test of time.

After exploring the gorge, we like to visit the adjacent Natural Bridge State Resort Park, home of more rock formations, including Kentucky's best-known sandstone arch, Natural Bridge. At 78 feet long, 65 feet high and 20 feet wide, this spectacular bridge can be reached by a short scenic trail.

The park's Hemlock Lodge, with its attached restaurant and tavern, is a convenient and welcoming place to end an enjoyable day of discovery. ●

POINTS of INTEREST

NOT TO BE MISSED

Zip and zoom! Soar over the gorge on an exhilarating canopy tour with Red River Gorge Ziplines. You can fly on five ziplines and walk three sky bridges. *redriver gorgezipline.com*

FUN FACTS

Along with being a designated Geological Area, the gorge is also a National Archaeological District and a National Natural Landmark, and appears on the National Register of Historic Places. A part of it is also designated as Clifty Wilderness, with 12,646 acres of rugged and wild forest landscape.

WORDS TO THE WISE

The rock features here are just part of the attraction. You can visit year-round to hike, camp, canoe, enjoy wildlife and other outdoor fun.

Although the cliffs here are beautiful, they can also be dangerous. Exercise caution and avoid cliff edges.

▼

Gravity-defying Rock Bridge Arch spans a fork of Swift Camp Creek.

Take a boat to explore the marvels of the flooded cypress forest.

STORY AND PHOTOS BY
CATHY AND GORDON ILLG

ATCHAFALAYA BASIN

FLOAT BETWEEN THE CYPRESS TREES INTO A VAST WETLAND,
A HAVEN FOR WILDLIFE FROM BIRDS TO ALLIGATORS.

IT HAD ONLY BEEN a few minutes since we left the dock, and we were already surrounded by stands of towering bald cypress trees rising up through the dark water.

A maze of narrow channels, shrouded by delicate curtains of Spanish moss, fanned out in every direction. How anyone can find their way through this bewildering and beguiling landscape is a mystery.

Our guide's Cajun accent drifted over the bayou as he reassured us that he could find his way back, and talked about his life on the Atchafalaya Basin, the largest river swamp in the U.S.

In 2006, a swath of Louisiana was designated the Atchafalaya National Heritage Area in recognition of the extraordinary natural environment and diverse culture. The heritage area follows the entire 140-mile length of the Atchafalaya River.

Most people visit the area for Cajun food, zydeco music and merriment, but the wildlife and scenery here can compete with any national park.

In spring the air smells like fragrant jasmine and honeysuckle, and surprisingly, mosquitoes are almost nonexistent unless you stay outside after dark.

While the basin is truly amazing, flood control, as well as transportation projects, have altered the landscape. Mississippi River floodwaters have been diverted into the Atchafalaya Basin, protecting larger cities.

NOT TO BE MISSED

Swamp tours of the basin shove off from McGee's Landing in Henderson. Most tours float beneath the twin spans of I-10, which was built to link this watery realm with the rest of civilization.

FUN FACTS

Atchafalaya Basin is home to more than 270 species of birds, 60 species of reptiles and amphibians, and nearly 100 species of aquatic life.

Louisiana has the highest alligator population in the country, with more than 2 million wild alligators. They can be found in ponds, lakes, canals, rivers, swamps, bayous and coastal marshes.

NEARBY ATTRACTION

Lake Fausse Pointe State Park is one of the region's oldest bald cypress groves. This 6,000-acre park sits on land that once periodically disappeared beneath floodwaters; levees on the park's eastern border now protect it from flooding.

▼

An American alligator at Lake Martin opens its mouth to cool itself.

But in the process the smaller communities such as Bayou Chene were inundated and abandoned, and the environment was affected and changed in many ways.

Yet the swamp is still a miracle of life. While many other large river deltas—including the Mississippi—are losing land, the Atchafalaya River Delta is actually growing larger.

The most fertile ecosystem in North America, it is more productive than any other river swamp on the continent. Twenty-two million pounds of crawfish are harvested in this region every year.

For a truly immersive experience, you have to see the wonders found in the swamp by boat. Interstate 10 crosses the river on the 18-mile-long Atchafalaya Basin Bridge, and the heritage area welcome center is located off the Butte La Rose exit. Begin your swamp expeditions here; you'll find that many swamp and wetland boat tours are launched nearby.

We decided to go on the water with Atchafalaya Experience, run by the father-and-son team of Coerte and Kim Voorhies. They've spent most of their lives exploring the Atchafalaya River. Coerte, a retired geologist, still enjoys getting out and seeing nature. They can maneuver the small boats into places I'd never have thought possible, with cypress trees touching both sides.

The boat tour immerses you in a mysterious world where much is hidden—alligators lurking under the water, frogs blending into the tree bark, and hawks and owls peering through the Spanish moss.

Sometimes there are so many dragonflies around that they use people as perches, and that's perfectly fine. Dragonflies don't hurt anyone, and they eat many of the bugs that do.

For landlubbers, one of the best places to experience the Afatchalaya Basin is Cypress Island Preserve, about 8 miles south of Breaux Bridge. Standing on the shore of Lake Martin, you can stare into an almost limitless expanse, where water and trees intermingle until they appear to become one.

The south end of the lake is home to a rookery of thousands of wading birds, including egrets, herons and spoonbills. An all-weather dirt road going around half of the lake gives visitors access to a boardwalk into the swamp where they can easily observe alligators. The birds like the alligators because they keep raccoons and opossums away.

You can spot wildlife just about anywhere in the preserve. Four armadillo pups once walked right up to us as we sat quietly. Access to parts of the walking trail may be limited during alligator nesting season.

If you're searching for an unusual travel destination, soak up the scenery and culture of the Atchafalaya National Heritage Area. You just might spot some interesting creatures among the cypress and tupelo trees. ☙

Lotus flowers ◀
float above the
surface of Millers
Lake in nearby
Evangeline Parish.

Lush trees cover the valley in shades of green.

STORY AND PHOTOS BY
LIZZIE HOWARD

CATALOOCHEE VALLEY

FIND THIS HIDDEN GEM WHERE ELK ROAM FREE ON THE NORTH CAROLINA SIDE OF GREAT SMOKY MOUNTAINS NATIONAL PARK.

GRIPPING TIGHTLY TO THE CAR DOOR, I nervously looked out the window as we wound along the mountainside, not knowing what was coming around the bend.

"Breathe, Lizzie," my husband, Jason, said, knowing I was scared of the drive.

"We're on an adventure!" Jason added in a reassuring tone.

The one-lane dirt road led to the Cataloochee Valley, a secluded and panoramic cove surrounded by majestic 6,000-foot peaks on the North Carolina side of Great Smoky Mountains National Park.

Cataloochee Valley is remote. There are only two entrances to the valley—one in Tennessee and one in North Carolina.

We knew very little about the place except that it is home to lots of elk. Jason and I love wildlife and wanted to see these animals grazing in the pastures, so we planned to reach the valley before sunset. After what felt like hours of driving, inches away from the mountain on one side and

NOT TO BE MISSED

For the best wildlife watching, arrive in the early morning or evening when elk, deer, turkey and black bears seek food and water. Remember that wild animals are unpredictable, so watch from a safe distance.

If catching wild trout is on your fishing bucket list, try the Cataloochee Creek and its tributaries. In fact, Great Smoky Mountains National Park has 2,900 miles of streams and is one of the last habitats for wild trout in the eastern U.S. Be sure to get a permit.

For a trail trek, Boogerman Loop is a popular hike that winds through an old-growth forest. Local lore says the trail was named for Robert Palmer, who owned this land and went by the nickname "Boogerman."

WORDS TO THE WISE

Give yourself at least a day to explore the Cataloochee Valley. Pitch a tent for an overnight stay. A primitive campground that accommodates tents and RVs up to 30 feet long is available in the warmer months.

▼

Nature lovers come to Cataloochee to see elk roaming free.

a drop on the other, the gravel road transitioned to pavement. Finally, I relaxed. The mountain road smoothed out before us with fewer tight turns and room enough to pass any approaching vehicles (neighborly driving is a must in these parts).

We stopped at the Cataloochee Valley Overlook, which took my breath away. I gazed out at peak after peak undulating on the horizon and lush stands of trees hiding the valley below.

Another couple had stopped to take in the scenery. We asked if they had seen any elk. They advised us to just keep driving and eventually we'd see them.

Slowly we descended the mountain, and the valley opened up to us. We came upon a herd of elk. These animals had all but disappeared in the valley due to overhunting and habitat loss, but in 2001 the Rocky Mountain Elk Foundation introduced a small herd.

These creatures have thrived here, and the herd has grown significantly in number ever since.

We meandered on, farther into the beautiful valley, passing the ranger station, Palmer Chapel, the Hiram Caldwell house and many other historic buildings.

Cataloochee is a small valley, so the atmosphere is intimate and authentic. It's a hidden gem within the park, and we felt as though it was shining just for us.

Deep in the valley, yet another magnificent view greeted us, this time as we looked up to the mountains and the bright blue sky above. We crept along as far as the road took us and spotted a lone bull elk. In awe of his massive set of antlers, we kept our distance and listened as he let out a bugle.

It was a stunning sight to see—elk dotting the landscape in their natural habitat with the mountains towering behind them.

As the sun set behind the vast mountain range, Jason and I sat together and watched the elk wander in the fields. We reflected on our adventure and the majestic views. We cherished our vacation together and looked forward to many more years filled with exciting journeys like this one.

The stillness of the evening air reminded me of a song in a Laura Ingalls Wilder book:

Golden years are passing by,
Happy, happy golden years,
Passing on the wings of time,
These happy golden years.
Call them back as they go by,
Sweet their memories are,
Oh, improve them as they fly,
These happy golden years. ❧

The Cataloochee Valley Overlook offers a view of the mountains.

The Linville River curves through a gorge beyond Wiseman's View.

STORY AND PHOTOS BY
DANA FOREMAN

LINVILLE GORGE WILDERNESS

TUCKED AWAY WITHIN A LUSH WOODLAND IS A RAW AND RUGGED LANDSCAPE THAT AMAZES ANY TIME OF THE YEAR.

HIDDEN WITHIN Pisgah National Forest in western North Carolina, you'll discover the 11,651-acre wonder known as the Linville Gorge Wilderness.

The powerful Linville River cut the 12-mile gorge; the river drops more than 2,000 feet through very rough terrain before flattening out in the Catawba Valley below. Jonas Ridge rises to the east, with Linville Mountain to the west.

The deep gorge has been called the "Grand Canyon of North Carolina" and "the big ditch." Cherokees called it *Eeseeoh* ("river of many cliffs").

Since this unspoiled wilderness contains about 39 miles of trails, make sure to stop first at the Linville Falls Visitor Center, located at mile 316 of the Blue Ridge Parkway. Pick up a trail map and then hike to Linville Falls, one of the most beautiful waterfalls in this forest. Located on the northern edge of the Blue Ridge Mountains, the falls marks the beginning of the wilderness area. One fairly easy trail leads to an overlook where the river can be seen barreling through a narrow canyon and dropping into the gorge below.

Stop at the U.S. Forest Service information cabin along the Kistler Memorial Highway, where you can access trail information and permits for primitive camping.

Some trails descend from the gorge's rim to the river; these trails will test even the fittest person. There are moderately strenuous hikes to enjoy as well, including an 11-mile portion of the Mountains-to-Sea Trail that runs through the Linville Gorge Wilderness on its way

NOT TO BE MISSED

Jewels worthy of this gorgeous setting, Upper and Lower Linville Falls cascade into the deep gorge like shimmering silver curtains. The broad trails that lead to the canyon overlooks here are among the most picturesque anywhere along the Blue Ridge Parkway.

FUN FACTS

The Linville Gorge is among the few places left to still resemble America's vanished virgin woodland. It is the nation's first officially designated wilderness area. In this pristine valley, massive white pines tower skyward beside lacy hemlocks, ruler-straight tulip trees and exotic-looking Fraser magnolias with leaves up to a foot long.

Spectators are drawn to Wiseman's View scenic overlook in hopes of seeing the "Brown Mountain lights," unexplained flickers along the ridge at night.

Mountain laurel blooms in spring.

to the Atlantic Ocean from Great Smoky Mountains National Park.

Black bears, white-tailed deer, hawks, bald eagles, ruffed grouse, wild boar, bobcats, foxes and coyotes thrive in the Linville Gorge Wilderness, as do snakes such as venomous copperheads.

During winter the area looks quite different. Bare trees and shrubs expose many rock faces, delivering a stark appearance. Rock formations along the ridges have interesting names such as Table Rock, Sitting Bear, the Chimneys and Hawksbill.

Spring and summer are inviting, with lush landscape in every direction. Rhododendrons grow alongside mountain laurel. But some consider autumn the prime time for visiting. It's true that the fall foliage often leaves me speechless.

After spending time here, you will have a new appreciation for the sheer beauty of this wild environment. ●

▼
This rustic cabin houses an information center for hikers and campers.

An iconic sight in the low country, weeping Spanish moss drapes from oak trees in Charleston, South Carolina.

STORY BY
HELEN TRUSZKOWSKI

GULLAH GEECHEE

A SEA ISLANDS CULTURE EMBRACES THE CRAFTS, FOODS AND TRADITIONS OF ITS ANCESTORS' RICH HISTORY.

ON A CHARLESTON SIDEWALK, I caught my first glimpse of Gullah culture in the form of a sweetgrass basket. A centuries-old craft that originated in Sierra Leone, these intricate baskets are woven by people who use techniques passed down from generation to generation.

The Gullah Geechee people are descendants of West African slaves who were brought to work on cotton and rice plantations. They live on the islands and in the low country along the coast of the southeastern United States, dotting a 400-mile strip from Pender County, North Carolina, to St. John's County, Florida. This area is known as the Gullah Geechee Cultural Heritage Corridor. "Gullah" refers to South Carolina islanders, and "Geechee" to Georgia islanders.

While they have preserved much of their African heritage and shared it with the world, the Gullah of South Carolina are disappearing, casualties of progress and development.

Today, fourth- and fifth-generation Gullah bring their history to life by

POINTS of INTEREST

REST STOPS

The legendary Rhett House Inn is within easy walking distance of Beaufort's historic district and riverfront. This 1820s Greek Revival beauty served as a recovery hospital for soldiers during the Civil War. *rhetthouseinn.com*

Dig in at Gullah Grub Restaurant, lauded by chefs from the late Anthony Bourdain to Martha Stewart. Locally sourced dishes include fish chowders, gumbos, and peach cobblers. *gullahgrub.com*

NOT TO BE MISSED

Gullah Heritage Trail Tours offer an informative drive through 10 Gullah villages. Led by a guide of Gullah descent, the tours give an intimate look at the roots of this rich culture. *gullaheritage.com*

Twenty minutes from Beaufort on the Sea Island of St. Helena, the Penn Center houses one of the country's first schools for freed slaves. With its museum and exhibits, the center is a key African American historical and cultural institution. *penncenter.com*

▼

Buy handmade sweetgrass baskets at the Boone Hall Plantation.

serving up flavorful dishes, weaving sweetgrass baskets and sharing their heritage in museums and tours.

In November 1861, the Sea Islands came under Union control. Wealthy plantation owners fled, leaving more than 10,000 African Americans on their own. Beaufort County became the first place in the southern United States where former slaves could begin to integrate themselves into free society. Those who stayed claimed land from abandoned plantations, opened businesses during Reconstruction and, as Jim Crow laws took hold, increasingly isolated themselves in communities along the corridor. Amid this shared experience, a new culture was born.

Like me, most visitors first encounter Gullah culture through sweetgrass

baskets for sale along the sidewalks of Charleston. Historically, though, this artistry belonged to infirm men put to work weaving large utilitarian baskets for the plantations.

It was on a chance visit to Hilton Head Island's Coastal Discovery Museum that I came across Gullah Sweetgrass Baskets Creations. Carrying on a proud family tradition, the gallery offers basket-making classes and a chance to watch these crafts being made by seventh-generation basket sewers Michael Smalls and Dino Badger.

Using just two tools—a pair of scissors and a sharpened spoon handle called a "nail bone"—the sewers follow no standard pattern. They showed me how the seagrass flows naturally into the shape of a basket. As each basket takes its own unique form, they charmingly name the basket based solely on how it looks.

Incomprehensible to most, Gullah's quick-paced Creole patois has stood the test of time. A complex, singsong mashup of English and African languages from the residents' native homelands, Gullah words can be traced back to the West African rice-growing regions of Senegal, Gambia and Guinea-Bissau, and as far afield as Guinea, Sierra Leone and Liberia.

As he shook my hand, Michael's parting words, "We bin ya, they come ya," left me with no doubts about his resounding sense of self and his strong Gullah bond. What Michael was saying was that the Gullah people belong here; the rest of us are just passing through.

It is only in recent years that the Gullahs' newly exhibited pride has been revealed to the rest of the world. Officially recognized as an international nation on July 2, 2000, today's Gullah people are starting to speak their dialect more proudly and to open businesses with "Gullah" or "Geechee" in the title.

As I traveled to the northeast, illustrious towns of yesteryear hurtled by—including quaint Port Royal and charming Bluffton—delivering me to the graceful oak- and mansion-lined streets of Beaufort, one of only a handful of spots in the U.S. that has its entire downtown designated as a National Historic Landmark. My sanctuary for the night was the immaculate Beaufort Inn.

As a sorbet-hued dusk settled in the courtyard, a crowd gathered and a dynamic ensemble named the Gullah Kinfolk broke into a rousing musical performance. Sublime storyteller Anita Singleton-Prather, backed by singing and dancing, channeled her Sea Island grandmother as she recounted her slave ancestors' long-anticipated freedom. Anita's commitment to

▼

At dusk, birds snatch morsels as fishing boats dock at Shem Creek.

Palm trees sway in Hunting Island State Park in Beaufort County.

unveiling the Gullah way of life was intoxicating. I wanted more.

I found it on St. Helena Island. It was a welcome antidote to so many of today's tourist-laden spots. I sensed a difference instantly as salty marshes perfumed the air. Flashes of a soft, long-ago South streamed past the car windows: clapboard cottages peeking out from pine forests, children waving at me from fields of wildflowers, and Gullah farmers at the roadside selling their farm-to-table collards and corn from pickup trucks.

Here, the 50-acre Penn Center, founded in 1862, is one of the nation's most historically significant African American educational and cultural institutions. As the first school in the South created for former slaves, it was where African Americans received a chance to be educated and gain skills they would need for life. As Penn School evolved into the Penn Center in the 20th century, it remained a crucial spot for education, community and political rallying. In the 1950s and '60s, civil rights leaders, including Dr. Martin Luther King Jr., met here.

Heading north from Charleston, I drove down an imposing kilometer-long avenue of silvery moss-draped oaks to the 738-acre Boone Hall Plantation & Gardens, one of America's oldest working farms. Founded in 1681, today's Boone Hall promises a rare and unflinching look at slavery, while celebrating the ingenuity of those who endured it. The history of the vaulted ceilings and hand-painted ceramics in the "big house" are all very nice, I realized, but they are only part of the narrative.

Nowadays, at least, the enslaved people who worked the land here are given equal billing to those who owned it. Passing through jaunty camellia, azalea and rose beds, I took an altogether more soul-wrenching walking tour of Boone Hall's slave

Visit the Dock Street Theater and St. Philip's Church on Church Street in Charleston.

cabin lane. Here the ins and outs of slave life are revealed in nine original brick cabins built between 1790 and 1810. While the walk was far from lighthearted, it was powerful to discover the slaves' mesmerizing resilience enduring in the live Gullah Theater at cabin 9. I heard Gloria's soulful voice before I caught sight of her, with her hair tucked under a bright turban, and a long apron whipping in the breeze.

As I sat with other visitors on a half-moon of wooden benches, Miss Gloria Ford's Gullah storytelling enthralled me. Her performance was emotional and impactful. Her vibrant songs, tales and playful anecdotes slowly peeled away the layers of Gullah heritage, which included a practice of painting their doors "haint blue" to ward off evil spirits and witches.

The National Trust for Historic Preservation placed the Gullah Coast on its list of most threatened places in 2004. I ended my heritage tour of the Gullah Geechee corridor wiser, with a new appreciation for those African ancestors who first shaped Gullah culture—and with a hope that it will be preserved. ✿

▼
Picturesque farms dot the countryside in this area.

STORY AND PHOTOS BY
LORI GRANT

BURKE'S GARDEN

PEDAL ALONG THE ROLLING HILLS IN THIS PASTORAL VALLEY TO REVISIT A SIMPLER WAY OF LIFE.

IF YOU LIKE TRAVELING to places with intriguing names, then put Burke's Garden, Virginia, also known as God's Thumbprint, on your list.

The first time that I visited, I imagined driving into a giant thumbprint cookie. While the aerial view resembles an extinct volcanic crater, scientists say the thumbprint was actually born of collapsed underground caverns.

Parachute into Burke's Garden and you'll land in Virginia's highest valley—a natural bowl ringed by Garden Mountain—about 3,000 feet above sea level. Tucked in the valley is an unincorporated community of tidy pastoral farms, a few churches and a general store. The closest good-sized town, Tazewell, is about a 30-minute drive away. Here you really do get away from it all.

No need to parachute, though, since there are two entrances to the valley. Only one of them, Virginia

Scenic Byway Route 623, is paved, and that is enough to keep the area secluded and peaceful. It's the perfect setting for rural cycling.

One morning I decided to try it out for myself. My husband dropped me and my bike off at the mill dam and I started out on the gently rolling loop road.

I leisurely peddled past grazing horses and cows, and curious llamas and camels. With each mile, I heard roosters, frogs and crickets, saw goldfinches, red-winged blackbirds and indigo buntings, and smelled fresh-cut hay, lovely wildflowers and, yes, whiffs of dairy air.

Cool breezes, warm sunshine and a sense of tranquility washed over me. Only a handful of cars passed by, and everyone waved.

After completing the 12-mile ride, I was hungry. Luckily, I arrived at Burke's Garden General Store just in time to try some piping-hot fried

▼
Share the road with Amish buggies when visiting.

NOT TO BE MISSED
Check out Burke's Garden General Store for some Amish-made food, see barn quilts throughout the area, hike part of the Appalachian Trail and stop by the Burke's Garden Fall Festival, held annually in September. The festival has farm-fresh food, crafts and demonstrations like apple butter-making and sheep sheering. *visittazewellcounty. org, virginia.org*

FUN FACT
Local legend says that the name "Burke's Garden" comes from when James Burke planted potato peelings by the campfire of a survey party in 1748, and later a crop of potatoes was discovered.

pies (apple, cherry or strawberry-rhubarb) made by the Amish ladies at the store.

The pies themselves were worth the trip to Burke's Garden. All of the mouthwatering food on the menu can be savored while relaxing on the store's porch swings and conversing with the neighbors.

The community is designated as a National Rural Historic District and is adjacent to the Appalachian Trail, for those who are interested in hiking.

The Burke's Garden Fall Festival is an annual celebration of hearty country food and handmade crafts. Fill up on apple butter and baked goods while you enjoy activities such as a barn quilt tour, wagon rides, living history programs, live music, farm demonstrations and more.

Whatever time of year you visit, Burke's Garden is a pocket of paradise for anyone who is looking to revisit a simpler time, with friendly local folks, picturesque scenery and quiet roads. God's Thumbprint will leave its own lasting impression on those lucky enough to pass through this pristine Virginia countryside. ●

LOVE

#LOVEVA   VIRGINIA IS FOR LOVERS

▼
Painted barn quilts are on display throughout the valley.

▼
Find 3 miles of trails through old-growth hemlock trees in Cathedral State Park in West Virginia.

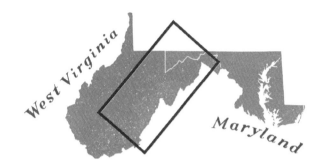

STORY AND PHOTOS BY
PAT AND CHUCK BLACKLEY

APPALACHIAN FOREST

IN THE ALLEGHENY HIGHLANDS, DISCOVER CHARMING MOUNTAIN TOWNS, ANCIENT FORESTS AND TOE-TAPPING MUSIC.

ERUPTIONS OF BLOOMING mountain laurel within the forests and open spaces of West Virginia's Allegheny Highlands usher in summer. Fields and forests ring with the sounds of returning birds, streams filling to their banks and the footsteps of hikers exploring the trails.

In this recreation paradise, it's easy for us to forget the people who made a way of life in these forests. So that we always remember, the Appalachian Forest National Heritage Area was created to conserve and promote the cultural legacy of the highlands in 16 counties in West Virginia and two in Maryland.

The story of the Appalachian Forest starts with the Native Americans who hunted here at least 12,000 years ago. It continues with German and Scotch-Irish settlers who in isolation developed forms of music, arts and crafts, and storytelling that endure.

Today, the descendants of those European settlers work, play, hike, hunt and fish in these majestic mountain highlands. The region is now a destination for nature lovers like us, outdoor enthusiasts and those who love the music and culture of the mountains.

Our first glimpse of Seneca Rocks, a stunning quartzite fin that rises 900 feet above the North Fork River, came as a surprise. Seneca Rocks is a must-see, if only for its sheer grandeur. Rock climbers test their skills on its face, but we decided to hike an easier trail to a platform near the top for a sweeping view of the valley below.

The national heritage area is full of stunning sites and vistas like these that leave us (and no doubt left the early pioneers) in awe. Although a logging boom in the late 19th and early 20th centuries clear-cut much of the forest, decades of thoughtful conservation have created wildlife refuges, wilderness areas, state forests and parks where folks come to appreciate the area's rugged beauty.

At the heart of the highlands is the mighty Allegheny Front, a long

POINTS OF INTEREST

NOT TO BE MISSED

Start your visit at the Appalachian Forest Discovery Center, where you'll learn about the area's past and efforts to preserve the woodlands. *appalachianforest nha.org/visit*

NEARBY ATTRACTIONS

Ride the Cass Scenic Railroad to the top of Bald Knob and go back to a time when logging was the main way of life.

Converted railroad beds are perhaps the railroads' greatest gift to these mountain communities. Catch the Greenbrier River Trail in Marlinton or the Allegheny Highlands Trail in Elkins, for example.

Have binoculars handy for some amazing birding at the Cranberry Glades Botanical Area in Monongahela National Forest. *fs.usda.gov/ recarea/mnf*

On the weekends, the restored Pocahontas County Opera House in Marlinton is packed for live performances of bluegrass, jazz and folk. *pocahontas operahouse.org*

Hike to Pendleton Point for a view of Blackwater Falls State Park.

escarpment that is home to West Virginia's highest peaks. On these heights sits Dolly Sods Wilderness, the highlands' crown jewel. It is known for rugged rock formations, sweeping vistas and hikes for every capability.

At an elevation of 4,863 feet, Spruce Knob is West Virginia's highest peak. It is the mid-Atlantic's premier dark-sky location and a wonderful spot to watch the sun rise. At the top is a short, well-developed loop trail and a stone and steel observation tower (be sure to bring binoculars).

You won't want to miss Blackwater Falls State Park. Not far from the Canaan Valley Resort, it attracts mountain bikers in the summer and cross country skiers in the winter.

In the park, as we walked down the boardwalk trail to the falls, we could

hear the thunder as the black water pounded and streamed into the canyon, sending a refreshing spray up toward us as we stood and admired the falls from an overlook.

For a glimpse of the ancient trees that drew loggers to this area, head to Cathedral State Park in Aurora. There, stroll the paths and meander among 500-year-old hemlock trees. We timed our visit to catch the summer rhododendron bloom, which beautifully decorated the scene. Similarly, a grove of 300-year-old hemlock and pine trees are preserved in Swallow Falls State Park in Maryland.

The region is dotted with mountain towns, or "mountowns," that embody the best of Appalachian culture. Of these, none represents the resilient spirit of modern outdoor communities

Elakala Falls softly spills into a canyon in Blackwater Falls State Park.

▼
In fall, the Cass Scenic Railroad tours the season's splendor.

better than tiny Marlinton, population around 900. The Greenbrier River flows through Marlinton, which is the seat of Pocahontas County. It has a vibrant visitor center, locally run shops, a restored opera house, cafes and parks. There you'll find the Greenbrier River Trail, a 78-mile converted railroad bed that is arguably one of the area's best rails-to-trails conversions. And the town is a gateway to the Monongahela National Forest, which is a great place to hike, bird, hunt or fish.

When in Marlinton, be sure to stop for lunch at the eclectic Dirtbean Cafe & Bike Shop, where you can watch mechanics repair bikes while you eat lunch (we love the wraps). The cafe also works with the Marlinton Art Center to offer classes in painting, glass fusion and ceramics.

Marlinton is also the jumping-off spot for many of our favorite outdoor destinations in the Cranberry Mountains to the west. We love to walk along the boardwalk among the cranberries, cotton grass and carnivorous pitcher plants in the Cranberry Glades Botanical Area, which protects the largest area of bogs in the state.

While there, we drove 23 miles of the 43-mile Highland Scenic Highway, traveling the mountaintops and descending to the Williams River, where riverside camping and fishing opportunities are found. Not far away is the Falls of Hills Creek Scenic Area, which features a boardwalk beside a mountain stream that leads to the first of three impressive waterfalls.

Of course, there are other mountain towns to explore, each offering a piece of Appalachian culture. In Elkins, relish traditional music, dancing and crafts at the Augusta Festival, a celebration presented by the Augusta Heritage Center every July. Elkins also boasts the Appalachian Forest Discovery Center and scenic railroads.

▼

Take a bike ride through the Paw Paw Tunnel in the C&O Canal National Historical Park.

But of all the communities, Helvetia was the most unexpected. It's less than an hour's drive along a paved, twisty road, and the journey is worth it. Built in 1869 by Swiss immigrants, this mountain village is well-preserved. Swiss influences are visible in the buildings, the cuisine, the culture and the festivals.

After a delicious meal at The Hutte Restaurant (menu items include Swiss classics such as *rosti*, sauerbraten and onion pie), we chatted with residents about their town and its festive seasonal celebrations. During Fasnacht, which is similar to Mardi Gras, people wear masks and burn an effigy of Old Man Winter. In April, the community gathers for ramp suppers, and in September, Helvetia hosts one of the oldest agricultural fairs in the state.

For pure nostalgia, head to Cass, a former logging company town that is home to Cass Scenic Railroad State Park. Riding on this railroad, one of five in the region, is a must-do. Built to haul logs out of the mountainous terrain, the Cass locomotives climb the 1901 grade, pulling open passenger cars as it chugs, chugs up the mountain. At the top, gaze out at the glorious view from West Virginia's third highest peak, Bald Knob. The town's structures look as they did during the logging industry's prime. Immerse yourself in the past by staying overnight in one of the company houses.

From our first visit, the Appalachian Forest had us in awe of the people, the views and the recreation opportunities. It is no exaggeration to say that it would be impossible to see it all in one lifetime. ◗

South Prong Trail leads visitors into the Dolly Sods Wilderness Area.

"**No matter how few possessions you own or how little money you have, loving wildlife and nature will make you rich beyond measure.**"

—PAUL OXTON

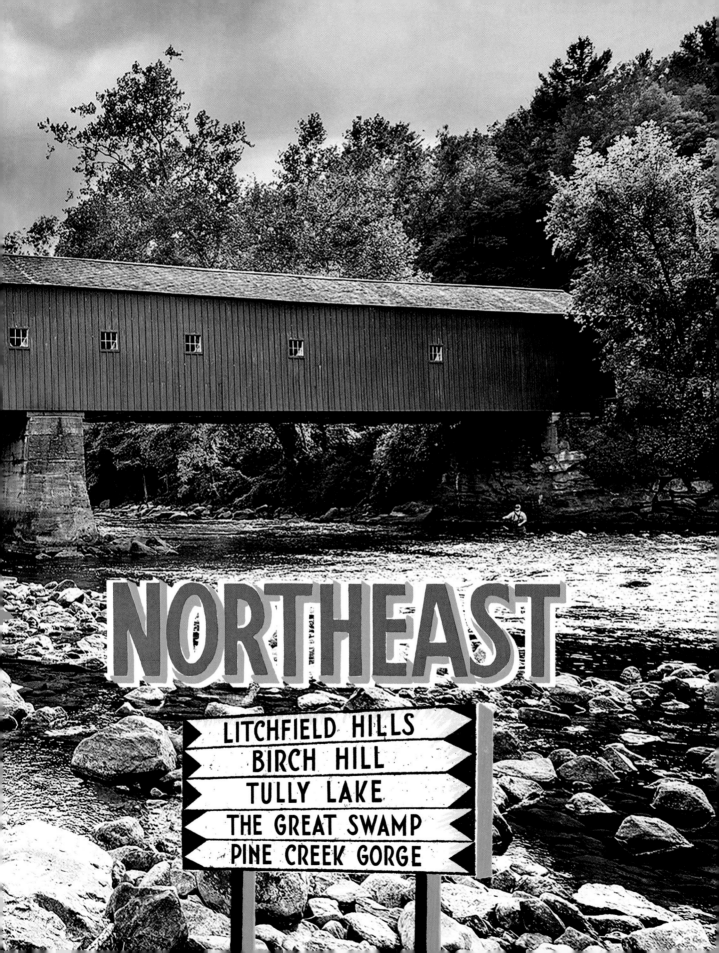

NORTHEAST

- LITCHFIELD HILLS
- BIRCH HILL
- TULLY LAKE
- THE GREAT SWAMP
- PINE CREEK GORGE

▼

Take the 8-mile loop around the lake at Lake Waramaug State Park, and make sure to have a camera handy.

STORY BY
PAULETTE M. ROY

LITCHFIELD HILLS

IN THIS AREA WHERE FALL IS BLESSED WITH VIVID HUES, YOU CAN EXPERIENCE THE IDEAL OF AUTUMN IN NEW ENGLAND.

IMAGINE A QUINTESSENTIAL New England fall in which forests full of birches, oaks, maples and other trees become awash in brilliant colors. Colonial villages, connected to each other by curvy country roads, dot the landscape, and their town centers brim with history and attractions.

This is Connecticut's Litchfield Hills, a region in the northwestern corner of the state known for its rural scenery. Exploring this area in autumn is a true delight to the senses. With really no particular agenda clearly in mind, my husband, Paul, and I simply open our atlas or turn on the GPS and wander up and down the back roads. We've encountered many babbling brooks, quiet ponds, hillsides of color and picturesque covered bridges and farms with well-kept barns. This is autumn in New England at its best—gorgeous and intimate.

Typical of New England, village greens, or town commons, are plentiful in the area, along with beautiful white-spired church steeples and colonial architecture going back at least 300 years.

Litchfield, incorporated in 1719, has a lot to offer visitors. Stroll along North Street and South Street to see stately homes that are National Historic Landmarks and buildings such as the Tapping Reeve House and Law School (the first law school in America). On Torrington Road, the crisp white facade of the First Congregational Church of Litchfield inspires visitors to pause and take a few pictures: It is one of the most photographed houses of worship in the region.

A little farther southwest is the town of Washington, which has three historic districts among the five villages of Marbledale, New Preston, Woodville, Washington and Washington Depot. Washington's green is known for its 18th- and 19th-century Georgian and Greek Revival houses. The New Preston

REST STOPS

The dairy store at Arethusa Farm is a popular place to stop for a scoop or two of old-fashioned ice cream crafted with fresh milk and cream. You'll also find milk, cheese, butter and yogurt for sale. *arethusaaltavolo. com/dairy*

NOT TO BE MISSED

Located in Cornwall, the West Cornwall Covered Bridge is one of only a few left in the state. Since 1864, folks have used it to cross the Housatonic River. Made of sturdy spruce, the bridge features a lattice truss design and is considered a New England icon.

In Falls Village, the railroad depot, bank, churches and homes give history buffs a glimpse of village life in the 19th century. Meanwhile hikers can catch the Appalachian Trail, which runs through town, and follow it to natural wonders. *canaanfalls village.org*

Set aside a few hours to explore the village green, museums, historic homes, churches and shops of Litchfield. *townoflitchfield.org*

St. Bridget's Catholic Church in Sharon adds to the fall splendor.

Hill National Historic District covers 210 acres, and its buildings give visitors a glimpse of what daily life was like when Connecticut was a colony. The Calhoun Street-Ives Road Historic District in Washington is a nationally designated rural agricultural district, highlighting 18th- and 19th-century farms with houses, outbuildings, fields, orchards and the typical New England stone walls.

To the west of Litchfield, Kent has a quaint town center where you can peruse art galleries and shops, indulge your sweet tooth at Kent Coffee and Chocolate Co., step back in time at the Covered Wagon Country Store, or take a moment to relax at the House of Books, an independently owned bookstore and literary landmark.

Whether you explore the area on foot, on a bike, in a car or gliding in a canoe, vivid autumn foliage is everywhere, and it is fantastic.

Because the Litchfield Hills are an extension of the Berkshire Mountains to the north, the area's topography lends itself to leaf peeping. Here you'll find the state's highest peaks, Bear Mountain and Mount Frissell, both in Salisbury. The terrain varies from steep rocky slopes to rolling hills.

Many hiking and biking trails keep outdoor enthusiasts of all levels challenged and happy. Spend a few hours on the rugged Appalachian Trail (47 miles of it wind through the state), or take a gentler hike or guided walk through one of the many state parks and conservation areas.

White Memorial Conservation Center's 4,000 acres and miles of trails—along with its natural history museum, live animals, bird sanctuary and educational programs—is a nature lover's gem with activities for the entire family. Or stop by Steep Rock Preserve in Washington for a peaceful stroll along the Shepaug River. For a quick trip, head to Dennis Hill State Park in Norfolk and drive to the summit pavilion for a 360-degree panoramic view.

Although it is certainly difficult to compete with the rugged beauty of the Appalachian Trail, the rivers, streams, waterfalls, ponds and lakes throughout the Litchfield Hills succeed.

The Housatonic River, whose name might have been derived from a Mohican word meaning "the place beyond the mountain," is the region's main waterway. The bridges that cross the Housatonic add to the charm and ambiance of the countryside. While traveling U.S. Route 7, Paul and I usually stop at two covered bridges: Bulls Bridge in South Kent, built in 1842; and West Cornwall Covered Bridge in Cornwall, built in 1864. Both are on the National Register of Historic Places.

The river moves fast from Falls Village to Gaylordsville, making it a popular destination for whitewater rafting. A more peaceful stretch, which runs from Falls Village to Cornwall Bridge, has some of the best spots for trout in the eastern United States.

A country road near Kent takes visitors on a fall foliage tour.

Opened in 1847, the Hopkins Inn overlooking Lake Waramaug features Austrian cuisine and access to the beach.

The Berlin Iron Bridge in Lovers Leap State Park spans the Housatonic River.

Lake Waramaug, a 656-acre paradise, beckons to swimmers, canoeists, kayakers, fishermen and leaf peepers. Drive along the shore for spectacular views of foliage reflected in the lake's still waters, or maybe rent a canoe for a peaceful afternoon.

Waterfalls are also prevalent, with Kent Falls in Kent Falls State Park on Route 7 being the highest at 250 feet, and perhaps the best known. Pack a picnic lunch and settle in at the base of the falls near the bridge that spans Falls Brook.

After you've had your fill of leaf peeping (if that's even possible), peruse works of art in galleries throughout the hills, most notably in Washington, Kent and Litchfield.

Those who love the theater can attend live performances at Music Mountain in Falls Village or the Warner Theatre in Torrington, which stages concerts, original theater productions and children's plays.

Or spend some time in the region's antique shops. Whether your interest is in Chippendale-style furniture or vinyl records, there's a shop for you in Litchfield Hills. Woodbury stands out as one of the top antiquing destinations because it has more than 40 shops, some housed in homes built in the 17th or 18th century.

When Paul and I are "on the road" in New England, most of the time we are in complete work mode, searching for scenic vistas, quaint country churches, covered bridges, sprawling farms or pristine waters flowing through deep forests. We are usually fortunate to find at least some of what we hope to photograph, and the Litchfield Hills did not disappoint us. We'll be back! ◗

STORY BY **PAULETTE M. ROY**
PHOTOS BY **PAUL REZENDES**

BIRCH HILL

HIKE, PADDLE OR SET UP CAMP AT THIS BELOVED SPOT
FOR OUTDOOR ADVENTURE.

LOCATED JUST A HOP, skip and a jump from our home in the forests of north-central Massachusetts, the Birch Hill Wildlife Management Area, including Lake Dennison and Otter River State Forest, is a perfect destination when we get the urge to view a sunrise outdoors.

This recreation area consists of state and federal land and encompasses more than 8,000 acres of public land and water. It was created in the 1940s, primarily for water storage behind the Birch Hill Dam on the Millers River, after destructive floods devastated many downstream towns.

More than 4,000 acres of reservoir land can hold up to 16.3 billion gallons of floodwater. This practical solution to prevent flooding opened up a parklike setting for outdoor enthusiasts.

Birch Hill is highly accessible via crisscrossed dirt roads and hiking trails from spring through fall. It's easy to see why it's a popular recreation area for fishing, mountain biking, bird-watching, hiking and photography.

Camping is also one of the major draws here, with two family-friendly campgrounds, Lake Dennison and Beaman Pond in the Otter River State Forest, each with swimming and picnic areas. Both are usually full throughout the summer season.

Winter offers an entirely different variety of invigorating activities, such as ice fishing, snowmobiling, cross-country skiing, snowshoeing and even dog sledding on unplowed roads.

Wildlife abounds, with mammals great and small, including red and gray foxes, fishers, deer and a growing moose population. Dawn and dusk are the best times for visiting the appropriately named Beaver Pond to catch a glimpse of the resident beavers, or the stealthy movements of great blue herons along the water's edge.

Canoeing the Millers River Blue Trail (from River Street in Winchendon downstream to just before the dam in Royalston) is another option for exploring the less visited parts of Birch Hill. All experience levels will enjoy the route. The river traverses forests, providing a "get away from it all" feel even if, like us, you're close to home. ●

Top: In the ◄
wetlands, blue
skies sparkle
on a tributary
of the Millers
River. Bottom:
Apple blossoms
welcome spring.

FUN FACTS

This area has many diverse habitats, including mixed hardwood and conifer forests, open fields, brush lands and shallow-water grass hummock marshes. An abundance of wildlife can be found here.

If you are looking to fish, the Millers River and the Otter River flow here, and each are stocked with trout.

Lake Dennison Recreation Area hosts the Massachusetts State Triathlon. Visit *maxperformance online.com* for details on registering or watching the action.

A sunset glimmers over Long Pond on the Tully River.

STORY BY **PAULETTE M. ROY**
PHOTOS BY **PAUL REZENDES**

TULLY LAKE

TAKE A QUIET WALK THROUGH A WOODED WONDERLAND
FULL OF WILDLIFE, WATERFALLS AND TRAILS.

TULLY LAKE AND TULLY RIVER are a world apart from the hustle and bustle of Massachusetts' most famous big city. Out here folks are fond of saying about their beloved state: "We're not all Boston. Escape to the west!"

As the crow flies, my husband, Paul, and I live less than 3 miles from the Tully Lake Recreation Area. There the seasons offer ever-changing opportunities to enjoy the exquisite beauty of this natural gem.

In addition to the river and lake, the recreation area includes dense forest, three waterfalls and a small mountain. Some of these sights are accessible by car, others on foot or by boat. The area is part of a large swath of protected rivers, lakes and forests in rural north-central Massachusetts that was created by a collaboration among federal and state agencies, conservation groups and individuals.

This extensive region for outdoor enthusiasts to explore began to take its present shape sometime after the great hurricane of 1938, when the east branch of the Tully River was dammed, and later when the lake formed.

Beginners will find excellent hiking trails along and around Tully Lake. A 4-mile loop trail mostly follows the shore, but also climbs to take you by well-known Doane's Falls on Lawrence Brook along the way. (The trail to the falls can also be reached by car.) Families especially enjoy the lake's walk-in, tent-only campground and picnic area.

Longer-distance hikers can take the Tully Trail, a 22-mile trek with a shelter to camp in overnight. This trail is the access route to many of the area's best-known attractions, including Royalston Falls, Tully Mountain, and a spur trail leading

FUN FACTS

This area covers 1,262 acres and is home to a wide variety of wildlife, such as songbirds, owls, waterfowl, deer, moose, fish, reptiles, and many mammals, including beaver, mink, otter, coyote, fox, raccoon, skunk, porcupine, rabbit and squirrel.

Enjoy mountain biking, camping, disc golf, hiking, picnicking, boating, and fishing and hunting in the appropriate seasons at the Tully Lake Recreation Area.

WORDS TO THE WISE

The Tully Lake Campground is open seasonally into October. Rent a site for an overnight stay or a canoe to explore the waters.

NEARBY ATTRACTIONS

The Birch Hill Dam is about 10 miles away and has plenty of trails and a river to explore.

The Quabbin Reservoir is also about 10 miles away. Four towns were flooded to create the Quabbin, and there is a mix of human and natural history to be found here.

▼

A hemlock forest surrounds Doane's Falls.

to Spirit Falls, the Ledges and Jacob's Hill. There's also a connection to the long-distance Metacomet-Monadnock Trail, which is part of the New England National Scenic Trail.

Water lovers enjoy boating, fishing, canoeing and kayaking on both the river and the lake, where there are several small islands that provide lots of nooks and crannies to explore. Paddle upriver to the beaver dams in the section called Long Pond on an early morning weekday, and you might see these busy animals or hear the sudden sound of a tail slap on the water; weekends get crowded. An unpaved and rugged biking trail also loops around the pond.

For the more contemplative visitor, there is plenty of space and solitude to indulge in nature study, photography and quiet woodland walks. The Tully River and Tully Lake area is a true treasure waiting to be discovered by those hoping to escape the bustle of the city. ●

▼
Take the Tully Trail to Spirit Falls, one of several waterfalls to visit in the area.

A canoe leaves no more than a ripple in the Great Swamp's peace and solitude.

STORY AND PHOTOS BY
SHARON MAMMOSER

THE GREAT SWAMP

WINTER ADDS A SPECIAL SENSE OF SERENITY TO THIS VAST
NEW YORK WETLAND.

BENEATH A CEILING studded with stars, two coyotes move soundlessly on the snow-covered river, their footprints adding to the tracks made by otters, red foxes, squirrels and other animals.

Twenty species of mammals live in the Great Swamp, which is among the largest freshwater wetlands in New York state. Little more than an hour north of Manhattan, this area around the headwaters of the Croton River covers more than 6,000 acres, stretching almost 20 miles through two counties. No signs announce its presence. In fact,

many of the area's 40,000 residents are unaware of its biodiversity and its essential role in the larger ecosystem. The Great Swamp provides clean drinking water to New York City, filters harmful pollutants and acts as Mother Nature's sponge to reduce flooding.

For more than 12 years, the Great Swamp was my backyard. I was blessed to explore its mysteries in every season, but winter was especially magical. When the water became a ribbon of white and the snow fell, the wetland became a blank slate on which every

POINTS of INTEREST

FUN FACTS

The Great Swamp provides an amazing value as a diverse wildlife habitat, scenic spot and critical aquifer recharge area. The wetland drains about 63,000 acres and spans two watersheds.

It's designated as a National Historic Landmark, a Critical Environmental Area and an Audubon Important Bird Area. Many rare and endangered species of plants and animals make the swamp home, including Atlantic white cedars and bog turtles.

If you are looking to paddle the area, there are 14 miles of navigable waters.

WORDS TO THE WISE

All-terrain vehicles, snowmobiles and motorboats are not allowed in the Great Swamp.

Be aware that ticks are most active during late spring and early fall, so wear protection.

Snow and ice make the swamp accessible to animals like this fox.

two- and four-legged creature left its own story.

While most people curled up inside their warm, cozy houses, I ventured outside to discover places that were inaccessible the rest of the year. In the shallow water beside the river, among the red maple and oak trunks, swirling air bubbles were trapped beneath the ice, creating rows of perfect circles and curves—art that rivaled anything I've ever seen in a gallery.

A Great Swamp winter quietly offers solitude, beauty and a unique natural classroom where new lessons are written daily. When the slow-moving river and surrounding wetlands freeze, the entire swamp becomes accessible to visitors willing to explore on foot.

I saw animals that most people see only in zoos. I watched muskrats foraging beneath the ice. I spotted bald eagles resting on snowy branches. From my many visits I learned that coyotes almost always travel in pairs, bobcats tend to move alongside of fallen trees, and raccoons frequently cross the river in favorite places.

Often when following mink tracks, I was surprised to see the small white-chinned animal suddenly appear, seemingly as curious about me as I was about it. Like otters, minks sometimes stand on their hind feet, making themselves taller as they study you studying them.

Otter tracks were everywhere, and I could see where otters had slid on their bellies into the open water. On full-moon nights, I ventured onto the frozen wetland and saw their dark shapes moving in the water as I listened to them noisily eating fish on top of the ice. Unlike beavers that slap their tails loudly in warning and then promptly disappear, the otters held their ground, squeaking at me to let me know they knew I was watching.

To recall my adventures with these creatures makes me smile, but there's so much more here to find here. The Great Swamp is also home to 36 kinds of reptiles and amphibians, as well as 62 butterfly species. More than 100 kinds of birds nest in the swamp, and 180 use it as a migratory flyway.

A true paradise for the senses, this remarkable wetland enriched my life daily. Its proximity to the nation's largest city is proof that humans and nature need not be in conflict.

The opportunities for hiking, cross-country skiing, kayaking and canoeing are wonderful here—but if you do visit the Great Swamp, please tread lightly. This special place deserves to be kept alive and intact. ❧

Dark trees cast ◀
their reflection
onto partially
frozen waters.

The forest tapestry reveals a glimpse of Pine Creek.

STORY BY
JILL GLEESON

PINE CREEK GORGE

ENJOY TAKING A BIKE, HIKE OR FLOAT THROUGH THE MARVELS OF PENNSYLVANIA'S GRAND CANYON.

ON A BEAUTIFUL summer day, warm and breezy with just a little humidity, the forest around me is lush and graced with evergreens as well as hardwoods—oak and maple in full leaf. Here in Pine Creek Gorge, I am just in time to catch the mountain laurel blooming. With dark, glossy leaves and gigantic clusters of pink or white blossoms similar to rhododendrons, mountain laurel is Pennsylvania's state flower.

As I hike, I feel the stress and strain of my everyday life slide from my shoulders, and I haven't even reached the edge of the canyon, which is where the real magic begins.

Tucked away in the Keystone State's north-central region, encompassing Tioga and Lycoming counties, Pine Creek Gorge is so spectacular that it has become known as the Grand Canyon of Pennsylvania. At 47 miles long, reaching 1,450 feet deep and a mile wide at most, it's far less imposing than the great cut slicing through Arizona. But this terrain is more hospitable—rich with vegetation, waterfalls and a range of trekking trails ideal for all skill levels.

Because I'm here for a few days, I opt to save the arduous 2-mile Turkey Path Trail, which leads from the eastern rim of the gorge all the way to the bottom, for my last day. Instead, I follow the shorter Overlook Trail.

Like the Turkey Path, Overlook winds through Leonard Harrison State Park, a lovely patch of land on the northern tip of the gorge. Across the valley sits Colton Point State Park, which is more rustic, with narrower roads and no visitor center.

As I reach the overlook on the trail, I think that there couldn't be any view of the canyon that could compare with it. I can see for miles, the glacially carved chasm unspooling into the distance. It's quiet, except for birdsong

REST STOPS

Located in a building constructed in 1862, the Wellsboro House Restaurant & Brewing Co. specializes in steaks, seafood and sandwiches. The owners also operate a craft brewery across the street. *thewells borohouse.com*

Three bed-and-breakfasts operate under the Bear Lodges name, including a Wellsboro inn and two rustic-themed but comfy properties located a stone's throw from the gorge's trails. *bearlodges wellsboro.com*

WORDS TO THE WISE

Situated at the entrance to Pennsylvania's Grand Canyon, the family-owned Pine Creek Outfitters has provided expert guide service and equipment rentals for gorge fun since 1984. *pinecrk.com*

▼

The Pine Creek Rail Trail goes from Wellsboro to Jersey Shore.

and the sound of the wind. I'm grateful that I chose to come here in summer rather than in autumn, when fall's colorful foliage brings more visitors to Pine Creek Gorge. All alone, I can imagine that I've gone far back in time to when the Seneca people roamed paths worn into the land, before the railroad and timber industry clear-cut so many trees that the area became known as the Pennsylvania Desert.

The fires, floods and landslides of that era eventually drove much of the native wildlife out of the gorge. Today, the second-growth forest shelters black bears, bald eagles, white-tailed deer, gray foxes, coyotes, river otters and many other animals. They have

plenty of room to roam—165,000 acres of Tioga State Forest surround the gorge. I don't see any animals on my hike, but I'm happy to know that the forest is their home again.

There's so much to do in Pine Creek Gorge beyond hiking, including rock climbing, backpacking, canoeing, fishing and even whitewater rafting. When Pine Creek is high during the spring thaw, it offers Class II and III rapids—fun rafting for grown-ups and kids alike. In summer, the water level is typically low, although Pennsylvania is well known for its fickle weather. Sometimes in late August the rains come, and then the swollen waterway is great to paddle well into October.

▼
Morning fog hangs over the forest in Colton Point, one of two state parks in the gorge.

▼
Pine Creek flows swiftly through Leonard Harrison State Park, which is on the east rim of the gorge.

▼

Gaslights line the streets of downtown Wellsboro, a popular place to shop, eat or stay.

After hiking, I head to the river with a kayak rented from Pine Creek Outfitters. The owners warned me that there isn't much water today, and it's true. I briefly get stuck on rocks in a few places. I'm not sorry I came out, though. The gorge is as lovely from the bottom as it is from the top. I am soothed by the sound of the gurgling water and the way the sun glints on it, also dappling the trees. I continue to feel this sense of ease after I trade in my kayak for a mountain bike.

Pine Creek Rail Trail, which was created from the remains of an old railroad bed, is used for many activities, including hiking, cross-country skiing and horseback riding. The best way to explore the trail, however, is on a bike. About 62 miles long, the trail offers a hard-packed gravel surface that is almost flat. Wellsboro Junction, named for the sweet little town near the gorge, is the trail's northern starting point.

I begin my biking adventure a bit farther south, at Ansonia, peddling quite leisurely toward the state parks. The canyon rises around me, the trees so thick they hide everything below their foliage. Somewhere to the right is Colton Point State Park; Leonard Harrison State Park is to the left. I've got maybe 12 miles to Blackwell, where the shuttle will pick me up. And then it's on to dinner in Wellsboro and a good night's rest before I hit the more challenging Turkey Path Trail the next day.

I find myself smiling as I think about this welcoming little canyon and all of its many charms. They are all well worth experiencing. ✿

"The clearest way into the Universe is through a forest wilderness."

—JOHN MUIR

A vast view from above of Leonard Harrison State Park in Pine Creek Gorge.